D0208220

THE
GIVING
PRESCRIPTION

᛭HE
GIVING
ᛔRESCRIPTION

A Personal Plan for Healing
Through Helping

COURTNEY CLARK

RIVER GROVE
BOOKS

This book is intended as a reference volume only. It is sold with the understanding that the publisher and author are not engaged in rendering any professional services. The information given here is designed to help you make informed decisions. If you suspect that you have a problem that might require professional treatment or advice, you should seek competent help.

Published by River Grove Books
Austin, TX
www.rivergrovebooks.com

Distributed by River Grove Books

For ordering information or special discounts for bulk purchases, please contact River Grove Books at PO Box 91869, Austin, TX 78709, 512.891.6100.

Design and composition by Greenleaf Book Group LLC
Cover design by Greenleaf Book Group LLC
Cover illustration: ©iStockphoto.com/pialhovik

Cataloging-in-Publication data
Clark, Courtney, 1979-
    The giving prescription : a personal plan for healing through helping / Courtney Clark.—1st ed.
    p. : ill. ; cm.
    Issued also as an ebook.
    Includes bibliographical references.
    ISBN: 978-1-938416-61-3
    1. Healing—Psychological aspects—Handbooks manuals, etc. 2. Helping behavior. 3. Social service. 4. Psychic trauma. 5. Bereavement. 6. Diseases—Psychological aspects. 7. Loss (Psychology) I. Title.
R726.5 .C53 2014
155.9   2013953584

First Edition

Other Editions:
eBook ISBN: 978-1-938416-62-0

This is book is dedicated to those of you who have been through the fire and have come out the other side somehow both stronger and kinder at the same time.

CONTENTS

ACKNOWLEDGMENTS

I am thankful to the doctors and staff at MD Anderson Cancer Center in Houston, Texas, and Columbia Presbyterian Hospital in New York City, particularly Dr. Merrick Ross, Dr. Robert Solomon, Dr. Philip Meyers, and their talented teams.

For the past several years, I have been honored to work closely with and for outstanding nonprofit organizations. The work done by passionate nonprofit staff members cannot go unrecognized. These people inspire me every day.

I appreciate the faculty and staff of the Saint Mary's University of Minnesota Philanthropy and Development program for all their help with the research that became the basis of this book.

My friends have kindly not commented on my absent mind and absent body as I plowed through this research and the subsequent writing. And when they did comment, they did so with love.

I have always been blessed with the loving support of family, who never thought there was anything I couldn't do. Except play sports. And they were right about that.

To my son, who embodies the spirit of survivorship with positivity every day: I am so grateful to have you in my life.

And finally, to the man who saw beyond my scars when he fell in love with me, who had to wonder if he would be widowed before we were married a year, who now walks in lockstep with me, hoping to heal the world alongside me: Thank you for being you. I love you.

Introduction

WRITING YOUR OWN
GIVING PRESCRIPTION

Kate was sexually assaulted when she was in college. She used all the resources available to her to help her overcome the trauma and went on to have a happy life. But after her daughter was born, she found herself reliving the trauma. She felt she needed something more to understand the meaning of her experience.

Jerry was a push-the-limits athlete who lost the use of his legs in a tragic accident. How could he accept his new normal—being confined to a wheelchair? He needed a new way to express who he was, to inspire himself to take action.

Dan and Mariella lost their baby very late in Mariella's pregnancy. They were heartbroken for months and unsure how to move beyond a wall in their healing. They each felt they needed a path out of their inner world of healing, but they were very different people.

And then there's me.

I was twenty-six years old when I was diagnosed with cancer. I had given back to other people for practically my whole life. But in one moment, my world turned upside down, and I had to rely on the help of others.

If you have faced a major life trauma, the odds are good that recovery has been a primary focus of your life ever since. Rebounding after a traumatic event takes time, and it is emotionally draining. It isn't uncommon to feel like life as you know it is over. You may feel as though you have to begin a completely new existence. Everything about this new life is strange and uncomfortable. As you navigate this unusual new world, you may feel that you'll never get back to the "old" normal you used to enjoy.

Posttrauma healing is an emotional and psychological journey. Your own trajectory from trauma to healing may not look like anyone else's. It may take more time than you thought, or it may take less. It may encompass more space in your brain than you want to give it, or you may be able to shove it to the back burner for periods of time. Everyone handles challenges differently, and everyone uses different skills to overcome adversity. There are, however, a few things that are universal about nearly everyone's healing patterns.

Psychologists have discovered that helping behaviors, like volunteering, donating, and advocating, are often a response to trauma, and that one of the final stages of the healing trajectory is the desire and ability to give back to other people. That shouldn't be too much of a surprise, since survivorship and philanthropy intersect: In undertaking either, we reveal an underlying desire to make the world a better place, to find equilibrium and a sense of fairness.

Philanthropic actions—like volunteering, donating, serving as an advocate, or starting a foundation—can help survivors find their footing after a traumatic experience. Studies have shown that survivors who participate in giving back recover faster than those who don't.[1] In fact, the experience of giving back after a life challenge is so helpful that for almost every kind of trauma (illness, loss of a family member, a combat injury while serving in the armed forces, living in a war zone, sexual assault), there seems to be a study suggesting that philanthropy could be helpful in overcoming it. Regardless of what you've been through, the benefits of giving back can extend to your psychological, emotional, social, and even physical well-being.

As a trauma survivor, understanding the ways philanthropy supports your healing can help you take full advantage of the benefits of giving back to others. That is my goal with this book: to help you find the right path of philanthropy to continue your healing. No matter what trauma you have faced, being generous to other people can play an important role as you move forward from your own adversity and seek to find meaning in it.

Why Use Philanthropy?

Kate, introduced earlier, suffered a terrible attack when she was in college eighteen years ago; she was sexually assaulted by a classmate. Kate's university offered free individual counseling at the time, as well as a rape support group. She took advantage of all immediate forms of help, eventually went on to have healthy romantic relationships, and married a man she met in graduate school.

Years later, when pregnant with her first child, Kate found herself reliving the trauma of the long-ago rape. Kate went back to counseling, this time as an adult with a different perspective. Her husband attended some of the sessions with her, and his understanding of her past deepened.

Several years after giving birth to her daughter, Kate was struck with the desire to help women who were coping with the aftermath of sexual assault. She attended volunteer training at her local rape crisis center and decided to volunteer to work the hotline two nights a month. On those nights, Kate often stayed up straight through the night until eight in the morning, spending up to two hours on the phone with a single client. Some of her calls were from clients who had just been assaulted that very night. Other calls came from clients just like Kate, who had encountered a trigger much later in life. Kate's own experience made her a perfect confidante for those callers, many of whom couldn't understand why their trauma was still coming back to haunt them. But Kate got it—she'd been where they were and felt what they felt.

Because Kate had both the background and the training to help guide sexual assault survivors in their moments of crisis, her role in the rape crisis center grew. She went from being a volunteer two nights a month on the hotline to running a face-to-face support group each week. As the volunteer in charge of the support group, Kate now facilitates healing conversations among sexual assault survivors. Sometimes, the people in Kate's support groups don't even know her history. They don't know why she knows what they've been through. But they can sense that she does.

Kate is an ordinary person like you and me. But she is a great example of how we can use our traumatic experiences to help others. Her story also clearly shows how we can use helping others as a springboard for helping ourselves—by making meaning out of our traumatic experiences. There are examples all around us of great works being done by people who once were in crisis. Everywhere you see pink ribbons or dimes marching, you are seeing symbols of good works begun as a response to a trauma.

Why does philanthropy help us heal? There are several reasons. When you give back, you're building new social networks and reinforcing old ones, and being with other people can alleviate depression and ramp up the recovery process. You may also gain an ability to make sense of the trauma that happened. Many survivors report that having a philanthropic outlet after a crisis made them feel like they could be a part of something larger than themselves, and they appreciated how giving back to others gave them the feeling that they could shield other people from experiencing the same fate.

Finally, one of the most important factors that makes philanthropy and volunteerism so successful in helping us heal after trauma is the way giving back allows us to take on a new role. When you are going through a crisis or an illness, or recovering from a major life change, you are often dependent on others. And although the words *victim* and *sufferer* are slowly being used less to describe people who have experienced traumatic events, they still linger in our vocabulary. They can impact the lens through which you see yourself. Thinking of yourself as weak can actually impede your healing process. Giving back to others is the ultimate statement of strength you can make as a survivor. You are taking an action that benefits not only you but also someone else who needs help. In taking action on behalf of a person who needs you, in serving as a "hero" to someone else, you can rid yourself of the passive victim identity.

In fact, the more you volunteer, the greater the emotional and psychological benefit you'll receive. The process of giving back to others will continue to pay off for years following your traumatic experience.

Any Form of Giving Back Can Help You Heal

All types of philanthropic activities—any form of volunteering, donating, or advocating—will aid in your healing process. There isn't any specific philanthropic role that is more psychologically healing than any other.

For some people, the most compelling work might be supporting individuals who are still freshly grieving. For others, it might be more fulfilling to help people transition back into their "new normal." Some people like to volunteer face-to-face, while others want to work behind the scenes. Certain survivors may want to enjoy the tangible payoff of building something from scratch, like an awareness event, a social media campaign, or even a foundation. Still others might want to tell their story to the world by becoming an activist or advocate.

No matter what type of volunteer role you feel drawn to, giving back can help you make the transition from your own trauma to a healthier, happier place. As a twenty-six-year-old public relations director, my little world was rocked by the diagnosis of invasive melanoma. I'd always worn sunscreen and had never visited a tanning booth. My diagnosis certainly wasn't "fair," the way trauma often isn't.

For weeks after surgery, I couldn't walk my dogs or dress myself. I couldn't lift my arms up to wash my own hair. I was dependent on other people in all the ways that a newly emerging adult can't help but resent. In the months that followed my diagnosis, I found myself wanting to reach out to other cancer survivors like me and listen to their stories. As a lover of stories, I found great healing in sharing with other people and providing moral support, a listening ear, the validation of a similar experience, or whatever they needed. I spent several years working with other young adults with cancer, providing them a safe place to process their diagnosis and their own mortality.

Ultimately, I knew I had a greater responsibility. See, it was easy for me to give back to other people. I had been raised as a volunteer at my mother's side. We would go to schools and put on puppet shows about inclusion and tolerance, or I would help her fold flyers about staying drug-free. We donated our old clothes and canned goods, and I watched my mom run from one volunteer committee to another. Since I had grown up giving back to others, it was easy for me to jump in and give back after my cancer diagnosis.

But deep down, I knew it wasn't that easy for everyone. If I hadn't been raised the way I was, I know I might not have thought about giving back to others as a way to heal my own trauma. A few years after I was deemed cancer-free, I launched a local volunteer movement in my community to help other young people start giving back, even if they thought they didn't have a lot of time and money to give. I had found a way to give back to others that was actually creating a cycle, by helping *them* give back to others, too. Creating a meaningful way to give back to my community through the nonprofit I founded was the ultimate act of survivorship for me. I can now leave behind a lasting legacy of people who have found their cause and discovered the power of helping others.

How This Book Can Help

Before you jump into philanthropic participation to bring meaning to your trauma and get back some of your personal power, there are a few key things to think about. If you want to make the best use of your personal crisis to benefit others, you need to first ask yourself a few questions, including when, where, and how you should start getting involved. This book is designed to help you answer those questions and find your own individual path to healing through helping others.

As I reviewed the research on philanthropy's benefits for the survivor population, I uncovered eight key issues that survivors need to think about before they begin volunteering or helping others. I've taken these issues and formed them into eight questions, each intended to help you find the right moment to step into a volunteer position and to help you choose the volunteer activity that best fits your needs and desires. We'll be exploring each of these in greater depth in a later chapter:

- Question 1: How much time has passed since the trauma?
- Question 2: Have you received any formal support?
- Question 3: What was the best support mechanism for you?

- Question 4: Are you able to tell the story of what happened?
- Question 5: How do you feel when talking about the trauma?
- Question 6: Do you still live in fear that something terrible may happen?
- Question 7: How do you express grief and stress in general?
- Question 8: In what ways do you see yourself making a meaningful difference?

Chapter 1 explores all the ways that helping behaviors can help you heal. It's good to understand how helping works so that you can build realistic expectations for your experiences. The rest of the chapters guide you through the process of exploring each of the questions, providing information about why the question is important and how to use your answers to make the best decisions for you and those you aim to help.

As you move through the book, I encourage you to answer these questions as honestly as possible. There is no right or wrong answer, just as there is no right or wrong spot to be in your healing process. The questions are meant only as a way to help you understand the expectations and challenges of all types of philanthropic activities so that you can find the right match. Getting involved with an activity that doesn't help round out your healing process is of no benefit to you or the people or organizations you are trying to help. By being honest as you answer the questions, you are on your way to finding a fulfilling giving experience.

In some cases, it also might be beneficial to ask people close to you, like family members or your mental health professional, to weigh in on your answers to these questions. Be sure you don't use their answers as a substitute for your own and don't give their answers any more weight than your own gut response. It can be interesting to see whether others have noticed anything about your healing process—the way you're always upbeat after a group therapy session, perhaps, or your frustration with certain types of activities. Sometimes an outside opinion is helpful.

Most important, be kind to yourself when answering these questions. Hopefully you have spent some time working on your own healing trajectory and are at a place where you may be ready to think about being helpful to others. Regardless of how far you have come, some of these questions might bring up uncomfortable memories of your traumatic experience. The work you do in this book is part of a learning process. The benefit comes from thoughtful answering of the questions you'll find within, not from agonizing over a specific step.

Use this book as your own personal tool. These questions are not designed to trick you or to imply any judgment of your healing trajectory. The information provided is based on research and case studies of actual trauma survivors who have used helping to heal. I'll share real-life stories about people who are using volunteerism and philanthropy to help them along their own healing path. The outcomes and choices suggested in this book, however, are only that—suggestions. Use your own best judgment when considering the questions. Only you can truly know which volunteer experiences will be meaningful for you. The point of this book is to serve as a guide and help you consider various points of view. (I've also constructed a flowchart that may help you arrive at the form of giving back that best suits you based on your answers to the questions. I recommend that you read about each question to understand the nuances of the process, but the flowchart can be a handy visual tool to get a preview of what might work best for you. Access it at www.thegivingprescription.com/flowchart.)

After working through the questions in this book, you will have an action plan for moving forward on your healing trajectory. The fact that you are working through this book means you have made a big decision to use your own trauma for the benefit of someone else. In the process, you will gain measurable benefits for your own healing, and you will be able to emerge even stronger than you thought possible.

Chapter 1

WHY HELPING WORKS

"Doing good is good for you." The phrase seems like such a cliché. Thankfully, it's more than that. While philanthropy is something we do to help people in need, helping behaviors like volunteering, donating money, and even just being a good citizen have been linked to many benefits for the giver, too. The benefits of giving back to others are now so widely known that we recognize the important role that philanthropy often plays in recovering from trauma. Giving back can have a deep impact on a person's emotional well-being, and trauma survivors—more than most—stand to benefit from that emotional healing. We benefit from giving back not just emotionally but also psychologically, socially, and even physically. During that critical healing time, giving back to others can help us recover our own footing. Studies of those suffering from trauma indicate that giving back helps survivors relieve depression and recover more quickly.[1] These positive benefits are not just a temporary distraction to take your mind off the pain, either. It appears that the positive effects of giving back to someone else last for years.

I was twenty-six years old when I was diagnosed with cancer. I had just moved across the country to a new state, embarked on a brand-new marriage, and started a new job. I thought I was building a life that was going to be stable and rewarding. Well, at least I got the rewarding part right. My dermatologist called me at 9:00 p.m. on a Sunday night. She had sworn up and down to me that the mole I wanted biopsied was benign. She had been wrong. I had malignant melanoma, and we had to act fast.

I was lucky. Because I caught the tumor early and we were able to attack it with just surgery, I had a short recovery that didn't require chemotherapy. Although my body bounced back relatively quickly after my short hospital stay, and I got to keep my hair, my thoughts took much longer to recover from a place of fear and uncertainty. When the first shoe drops at age twenty-six, you're left with a lot of years that you could spend waiting for the other shoe to drop. I made a decision several months later that I wasn't going to approach my battle with cancer as a horror film, something I could peep at through my fingers only when I had gained the emotional strength, or when the soundtrack didn't sound like anything too ominous was about to occur.

I went on the Internet and found out about Planet Cancer, an online support group for young adults who had been diagnosed with cancer. Another young adult survivor had started the site several years earlier, and it was now thriving, with thousands of participants worldwide. There were several participants on the site who shared my diagnosis of melanoma and prolific message boards where almost every question you could ever have about cancer as a young person was asked and answered. It quickly became obvious that the site shared my outlook on the cancer experience—if you don't find something to laugh about, you might as well be in a Lifetime movie of the week. Young adults fighting and surviving cancer congregated on the site and laughed and cried together regularly.

I hadn't even been out of the hospital a year when I sent my resume to Planet Cancer. I knew they were located in my state, and I was eagerly willing to relocate to work for them. When I joined the staff several months later, I knew I had found a place where I could help other survivors feel less alone about their cancer journey. I thrived as I wrote funny stories about going through my first CT scan, joked with other survivors about their scars, and learned all about the ridiculous things you sometimes do when you have "chemo brain."

In working with other young adults with cancer, I became fascinated by how my participation seemed to ease my fears and improve my outlook. Science confirmed it for me. One decades-long observational study of widows that was completed in 2007 found that the more the widows participated in formal service activities after they were traumatized by the death of their spouse, the better their overall well-being became.[2] It seems that finding a way to give back as much as possible, without overwhelming yourself in the process, makes for the highest psychological health scores for trauma survivors. Interestingly, the same study also found that the widows with the very highest feelings of well-being were the ones who had already been volunteering before the trauma happened, but who then increased their involvement afterward.

You can't go back in time and start volunteering before your trauma if you weren't already doing so. But you can still reap the benefits of service to others by making giving back a part of your life now.

What are the potential benefits of being a philanthropist? Researchers who study altruism have found several major benefits, each of which we'll explore in this chapter. They include

- increased personal connections;
- a great internal feeling often dubbed the "helper's high";

- a sense of purpose in life;
- rediscovery of a sense of personal power, which may have been diminished in the course of the traumatic experience; and even
- practical benefits, like a way to fill the hours of the day.

Let's take a look at these powerful rewards of incorporating philanthropy into our lives after a traumatic event—starting with personal connections.

Personal Connections

Philanthropy can provide easy access to one of the greatest tools for healing: connection to other people. Ervin Staub, a psychology professor who himself survived living in Nazi-controlled Hungary as a young Jewish boy, recognized that connections to others— "loving connections," as he calls them in *The Psychology of Good and Evil*—are critical in determining a person's ability to withstand trauma. Research about survivors in postwar Yugoslavia found a similar benefit to personal connections. In Yugoslavia, survivors of all ages, even children, were involved in a cohesive social effort to rebuild the community using personal ties. "Trauma does not occur in a social vacuum," the researchers write, "and cannot heal without supportive social interactions."[3]

Giving back to others can be a valuable way to have a bonding experience with the people who are already close to you. If you and your friends or family care about the same cause, consider how close you'll feel if you substitute a service activity for your normal night out having dinner. Volunteering together becomes a valuable shared memory because of the effort you expend and because of the uniqueness of helping someone else. Bringing family members—especially children—with you to service activities is not only a thoughtful way to bond but also a great way to start deep conversations about values, goals, and gratitude. Sharing your passion for a specific cause with those people closest to you can seem intimidating, but it ultimately leads to deeper relationships.

As you volunteer with your family and friends, you will find that you're uniting against a common enemy—the trauma you faced. At the same time, it also gives you a new task to face together, now that the initial trauma is over. While you may have all been united against your original trauma in the first place, only one of you (that's you!) was fighting the battle, and the rest of your friends and family were the support system. Now, the playing field can be more level, and all of you can band together in a common experience.

When we commit to an organization as volunteers, donors, or both, we are likely to also meet new people: the staff of a nonprofit, other volunteers, and the clients a chosen organization works to serve. And almost always, the people you're working alongside will share your goals, your values, and your conviction about the cause. In a study on breast cancer survivors, researchers found that survivors felt the most supported through their experience when they had "the opportunity to interact with and help others as well as develop new friendships."[4] These personal connections with new friends who share your cause can normalize your experience because they often have shared the same or similar experiences. Even fellow volunteers who haven't shared your exact trauma at the very least value your experience and value making the world a better place for others; otherwise, they wouldn't be giving their time to the cause.

Making brand-new personal connections can also be helpful to trauma survivors because these are people who didn't see you at your lowest point. As you struggled through your crisis, your friends and family functioned as your support network; they saw you as someone they needed to help. Some of them may be able to shift their perception of you right away, but some may have a hard time figuring out a new way to relate to you. They may be stuck in the old habits of connecting with you, which probably included some version of caretaking. But when you make new connections through new activities, you have the chance to spend time with people who don't have a memory of you in the neediest phase of your life. They were never your caregivers and won't relate to you as someone they need to take care of.

The Helper's High

Scientists have proven that giving back to others produces the exact same feel-good chemical reaction as an intense workout. The physical and emotional euphoria you feel after exercise is caused by a release of endorphins in your brain, and the same thing happens when you help someone else—resulting in the helper's high. Those endorphins help dull physical pain and elevate your mood.

Researchers have shown that volunteers' heart rates and blood pressures drop when they are in the act of doing a good deed. It's as if your body is cooperating in helping you give back to others. It feels so good physically that you want to keep coming back for more. Some studies suggest that—just like exercise—it doesn't take a lot of volunteering to reap the healthy benefits. As little as two hours a week produces the amazing biological effects that contribute to the helper's high.

Trauma survivors can particularly benefit from this kind of endorphin release. In the wake of your adversity, you may be suffering from lingering feelings of depression or malaise, and experiencing the helper's high could effectively combat that downward chemical spiral by producing feelings of happiness and usefulness. And the helper's high doesn't require overthinking. On your healing trajectory, you may catch yourself mentally working through the implications of everything that happens to you. As trauma survivors, we try to use our analytical minds to make rational decisions as much as we can, because what happened to us often feels irrational. But the great thing about the helper's high is that it doesn't require overthinking or intellectual buy-in in order to work! The helper's high is a biological response, and it's going to deliver endorphin goodness whether you realize it or not.

If a little helping is good, more seems to be better: The more hours a survivor volunteers, the better he or she copes. The aforementioned study of widows who volunteer[5] confirmed that more volunteering is better, provided you don't drive yourself crazy through overcommitment. So carve out some time in your schedule, and make it meaningful time. Human beings value what we prioritize. Don't do the bare minimum; instead, make that time something achievable but a little bit of a stretch. The same advice goes for monetary donations. Find an amount that is meaningful to you—something you'll notice but that won't leave you unable to pay your bills. When you give back at the upper end of your ability, you'll be maximizing your psychological benefit and the helper's high.

Another aspect of the helper's high is the intellectual reward of breaking out of your routines. In daily life, you may find yourself doing the same activities over and over again, as though by rote memorization. Have you ever gotten home from the grocery store and found all the necessary items in your sack, with no memory of shopping for them? Or driven home from work on autopilot? The same kind of memorized pattern can happen when we're in the middle of a traumatic experience. We might adopt patterns that worked to get us through the trauma, but now those habits don't serve us any more.

If your trauma foisted major changes on you, you might have adapted to those changes, but you're probably a little bit resistant to changing yet again. That resistance can leave you with behavioral adaptations you created to deal with your trauma that aren't really relevant to your life as a survivor. If those adaptations are no longer relevant, if they're holding you in the trauma mode, it may be time to shrug off the limitations they're placing on you. By taking on a new task, especially one about which you are passionate, you are triggering a new set of pathways in your brain. A new activity like volunteering brings with it excitement, apprehension, and nerves—sensations and highs you might have forgotten about in your repetitious daily life.

Finding a Purpose

John Walsh was a regular Joe—right up until the day his son was kidnapped and murdered. Walsh was working his hotel management job on the day his six-year-old son Adam was abducted from a shopping mall. In the year following Adam's disappearance, Walsh went from everyman to crusader. He founded the Adam Walsh Child Resource Center for legislative reform and was the driving force behind the Missing Children Act of 1982 and the Missing Children's Assistance Act of 1984.

Because of his efforts, John Walsh became a well-known face associated with preventing crimes against children. In 1988, his face became even more famous with the launch of the television show *America's Most Wanted*. The television platform gave Walsh an even broader reach, and the show played a role in the capture of more than one thousand criminals during its history. By giving back and helping take dangerous offenders off the streets, Walsh had found a purpose that helped him through his trauma.

Giving back to others or working for a cause can help us make meaning out of the trauma we experience. Like John Walsh, survivors of trauma are often driven by a desire to become part of something bigger than themselves, as a way to make an impact on the root cause of the trauma.[6] Joining a movement of change gives survivors a way to work toward a better future. Volunteering or other forms of philanthropy, such as starting a foundation, can be an effective way to get that experience—to discover or deepen our purpose. Real-life experience from nonprofit staff on the front lines and scientific research demonstrate that the volunteers with the strongest commitment to a cause are those who have faced similar obstacles themselves. More than any other volunteer, the trauma survivor has a vision for a future in which no one else suffers the way he or she had to.

Finding your cause can ignite a fire in you that perhaps your job or career has not inspired. It gives you something new to talk about with family, friends, and colleagues. It brings you a peace you may not have experienced since before the trauma occurred. When you find the cause that speaks to you, you may realize exactly how much your help is needed. And when you discover how much of a difference your work can make, and how important you can be to solving a problem you care about, you may find that purpose, or grow closer to it.

If you find or deepen your purpose through philanthropy, you may uncover a way to put your trauma in perspective. In order for this to be successful, it's helpful if you, the survivor, think about what forms of giving back are most likely to help you find meaning in your trauma. Which activities feel meaningful, and what are the meaningful outcomes of those activities? It's important to realize that meaningful participation means different things to different people and to realize that only *you* can determine what purpose and meaning you'll uncover through giving back.

Trauma survivors who have discovered a purpose, who have made some meaning out of the experience, have made it past some of the early healing hurdles. You may recall in those early days how the people around you said things like "I don't know how you made it through," "I couldn't have done it," or "You're so strong to have gone through what you went through." Of course, it's good to keep in mind that you *are* strong. You're a survivor. But it's hard for outsiders to understand exactly how and why you keep putting one foot in front of the other each day, in the face of what may be serious adversity. And yet you do. You may feel like you don't have another choice. Maybe you wonder how and why you do it, too.

This is where activities like volunteering, donating, and giving back can play an important role. In helping someone else, you are creating a reason to get out of bed every morning. A study of people with severe congenital health issues revealed that having a sense of purpose in life was more important to them than factors like autonomy or personal relationships with others.[7] Even study participants who had lost much of their functioning and their basic ability to take care of themselves thought they had gained a critical benefit because they found their "calling."

This calling, this sense of purpose, is likely why trauma survivors appear so strong to the outside world. We don't have a choice of whether to keep putting one foot in front of the other, because we have made the choice to survive. We are driven by a sense of purpose that is tied to our survival. Where other people may feel a general calling to accomplish something important, we survivors have seen the need and the fear firsthand. We have experienced it. Our sense of purpose may drive us to heal not only ourselves but also others. Once we have been through a trauma, taking hold of that sense of purpose and developing it to include others can be an important part of our healing.

When working for a cause, we have the chance to discover what truly inspires us, what makes us tick. Unlike our regular jobs—where we often have to make choices based on what we've been trained to do, or what we can make money doing, or what kinds of jobs we can find—volunteering allows us to make choices based on who we are and what's important to us. Our passion is the only thing that matters when we're giving our time to help someone else.

The activities that give you a sense of purpose will be unique to you. Some of your purpose may be driven by your experience and perhaps a desire to make life better for other people in the same position. Some of your purpose, however, may be a passion that has been lurking in the background for your entire life, even before the trauma, waiting for the right moment to surface. Whatever you derive your sense of purpose from, know that it can become deeply important to your healing experience—and that giving back is an excellent way to begin exploring it.

Regaining Your Sense of Personal Power

Helping also works to heal by pulling us out of the cycle of victimhood and allowing us to regain our sense of selfhood. When we are in the middle of a crisis, we are in dire need of help from others, particularly in the early days, weeks, or months after some form of trauma. We need our friends, family, doctors, counselors, neighbors, and colleagues to bring us food, do our laundry, help us adjust to a new lifestyle, hold our hand when we're feeling lost, and so on. I remember coming home after my first surgery at the cancer center and having to call a neighbor to come over and pull all my canned goods off the high shelves and relocate them to the bottom of the pantry. I couldn't even reach my arm up high enough to grab myself a can of Campbell's Bean with Bacon soup (a stellar comfort food, in my opinion). Even the words we use to describe people in these stages can be disempowering: *victim, patient, sufferer.*

Volunteering helps us complete the cycle of healing by transitioning us away from the victim mentality. This isn't a short transition, and it requires more than just a change in verbiage. It requires first a shift in self-talk, then a shift in persona, and then some concrete actions.[8] One of the most obvious and simple (though not always easy) ways to leave the victim persona behind once and for all is by taking on a completely new persona: that of hero.

Viktor Frankl is a hero to many. Frankl gets a lot of credit for introducing the rest of the world to what it means to embody the spirit of a survivor. His book *Man's Search for Meaning* is a widely read account of his time in a World War II concentration camp and of the strategies he used to survive there. Frankl detailed how those survival mechanisms later translated back to the "real world," when he had to cope with life after liberation.

Frankl suggests that one of the most powerful strengths left to him, after all of his dignity, choice, and power were stripped away, was that he could choose his attitude. He found that in whatever little way he could support others in the concentration camp and keep up an attitude of service, he was actually exerting his personal power over the situation. This insight can be helpful for survivors of any traumatic situation. Even when all your power appears to be gone and when the things that once made you powerful have left you, you can find a new power. And it can come, as it did for Frankl, in the form of helping someone else.

Why is community service so therapeutic for survivors? When you give something back to others, you are able to see yourself through a new lens. In many cases, survivors lose their sense of identity. When I met Jerry, for example, he was making the transition from life as a push-the-limits, no-fear athletic type to life in a wheelchair. He'd had an accident that left him without the use of his legs, and he had to make a few major changes in order to achieve a new normal. While Jerry retains all the great character traits he had prior to the accident, he also had some pieces of himself that he just couldn't get back, like his identity as an extreme sports competitor.

Jerry had to find a new way to be who he was inside—he

couldn't rely on the same outlets he had before. So he decided to take up Paralympic competition, and eventually became a medaled competitor. Today, he travels the world speaking on the transition from his life before the injury to his life now, giving back to others by sharing his inspiring story. The reality is that trauma can sometimes take away pieces of our life that we loved, but we, like Jerry, don't have to sit around for a long time with a giant, gaping hole in our lives left behind by our limitations. Philanthropy can offer a great way to fill the gaps that trauma leaves behind.

Eventually, we all want to make the transition from victim to survivor, but research shows that psychological healing in survivors does not happen until the survivor and his or her support system see the survivor as capable once again.[9] When you can reach back and help someone else out of the hole that you yourself have been in, you are truly strong. You not only survived that situation yourself, but you have taken action on behalf of someone else. This process helps you begin to define a new sense of identity and self based on the support you're giving others.

Jessica was devastated when she lost her husband at the age of thirty-six. Though they both knew his death was coming, she was unprepared for the void left in her spirit when she had to face the world alone as a widow. Everything around her seemed to be a reminder of him, from the music that had soothed him through his illness to the shoes she spotted in a store window and knew he would have loved. When people told her, "You are young. You'll love again. You'll find someone else," she thought her heart would break in two. Inside, she knew that she had already loved and lost her soul mate.

When Jessica first started seeking support, she found herself feeling even more adrift; many groups for surviving spouses are aimed at older people. Jessica felt alone and different from the other widows. As the months went on, friends connected Jessica to other young widows and widowers. Before too long, Jessica became a leader among her peers because of her thoughtfulness and compassion when it came to dealing with the newly bereaved. One day over breakfast, Jessica told me, "In helping these other people through the first few months, I realize how far I've come myself. These days, I only sort of half-remember going through that phase."

Jessica didn't think of herself as a leader. In fact, she thought she didn't have much to teach her peers who had also survived the loss of a spouse. But as she reflected on the new widows and widowers she mentored, she realized that they needed her help, her strength, and her insight. She had made it through her loss and was now prepared to help others. Her new identity as a leader revealed just how far she'd come.

To cope with your own trauma, you likely had to be stronger than you ever thought possible. You had to have determination and hope and an insistence that you could survive. You went from relying on others to being able to rely on yourself. But even that self-reliance may not always be quite enough. To complete the cycle of healing, it helps to shed the victim role completely. Being a support system for someone else, using your newfound strength for someone else's benefit, can be one of the fastest routes to leaving that victim persona behind.

Practical Benefits

While you are busy coping with the emotional and psychological elements of healing from your trauma, you may be experiencing some more immediate, tangible issues, too. For one, following a trauma, your days might seem almost empty compared to the hustle and bustle of your former life, a fact that is even more true if you were working before and now aren't any longer. If you feel that your trauma has set you apart from the world, use your volunteer role to catapult yourself back into it. Philanthropic activities can give you a way to get out of the house and do something with your time rather than letting your mind dwell.

Many survivors also cope with another concrete issue: the loss of a job and the looming pressure to find another. Yet again, giving back can help. Volunteering is a perfect way to try out new skills with no pressure. If, at your last job, you found yourself needing to brush up on your technological skills, for example, offer to help a nonprofit clean up their database. You'll get real-life experience and can potentially work on a project that looks great on your resume. Plus, that increased energy of the helper's high can give your attitude a bump during your job search and put you more at ease during job interviews.

As an extra bonus, volunteering can better your skill set and help you network with people who might hire you. Volunteering also gives you great stories to tell when you are interviewing or networking and provides a way to share stories about your passions without forcing you to talk about your own trauma. Give yourself somewhere to go every day and line up activities that will fill up your time, enrich your skill set, and give you valuable experience.

Crisis and Giving: Distant Cousins

Trauma can leave you feeling emotionally drained, selfish, and just plain incapable of sparing a passing thought for anyone else. Just when you think you have the least to give, you might actually be wrong. Studies of various populations show that people who have survived traumas of all types are in fact *more* likely to be philanthropic—to give freely of their time, money, and talents—than their peers who have never experienced a crisis situation.[10] It appears that people who have touched suffering or come close to it, those who know firsthand what it feels like, are the most likely to reach out and help others avoid it.

One obvious reason for increased generosity among trauma survivors is that we survivors now understand the needs of the traumatized population, and we feel responsible for stepping in and helping. We also are emulating the compassionate helpers who guided us through our own traumatic experience. In giving back to others, we are giving a nod to their hard work and paying it forward on their behalf.

By stepping into a helping role, you also complete what has almost become a rite of passage for survivors. Because survivors give back at a high level when compared to the general population, it is becoming widely acknowledged as an important part of our healing trajectory. But this expectation that trauma survivors will give back—this "positive pressure"—is part of what can encourage trauma survivors to give back in inappropriate ways. You will want to be a part of this rewarding experience that so many other survivors talk about, but you need to be sure you're doing it in the way that works best for you—not in the way that worked for the survivors around you; not in the way that someone helped you while you were working through your trauma; not in the way that worked for your coworker Mary. In the following chapters, we'll discuss in greater detail how you can be sure that you are choosing the right path for you.

As we've seen, giving back to others can play a critical role in your own healing. Don't ignore that twinge in your gut reminding you that there are still other people out there who could use your help. Following that impulse could be the greatest gift you give yourself. As you read on, you'll find the right path to helping others, which will, in turn, help you make the most of your own healing process.

Chapter 2

TIMING IS EVERYTHING

I once worked at an animal welfare nonprofit that did rescue, adoptions, and veterinary care. We had a dedicated staff, but the realities of nonprofit funding meant that volunteers—albeit trained and loving ones—were responsible for a great deal of our animal care. The volunteers walked and played with the dogs and cats, raised abandoned foster puppies and kittens by hand, and helped families find a perfectly matched pet to bring home.

One volunteer interview stands out from among the rest in my memory. This woman was a passionate animal lover and was eager to begin her volunteer duties. At her interview, however, she revealed that she had recently had to put her elderly cat to sleep. The experience of losing a beloved pet is traumatic for many pet owners, and this woman was no different. She wanted to fill the kitty-shaped hole in her life by giving back to the homeless cats at the shelter. After half an hour, however, she was unable to control her sobs, even when we went to visit the cat play area. Her grief for her lost cat had overwhelmed her to the point that she couldn't even enjoy playing with the cats during her volunteer interview. Her wounds were still too fresh.

In the research on healing after trauma, one of the most important predictors of a survivor's readiness to serve as a volunteer is the simple question of psychological distance. When there is a significant amount of time between the initial trauma and the taking on of a volunteer role, the experience of both the volunteer and the clients with whom he or she works is more likely to be positive. If you are still in the early stages of grief, you are emotionally vulnerable and may be unprepared for the burden of some types of helping. The experience of trauma itself is not enough to ensure that you are ready to help other people through it.

To offer support to others, you have to be far enough along in your own healing process. If you aren't—if you don't wait long enough before giving back—you won't be a particularly good volunteer, *and* you run the risk of disrupting your own healing. You will miss out on the benefits described in chapter 1. After most major traumas, you must have some kind of distance between yourself and the event; you must be on solid enough ground before you can be helpful to someone else.

Because the issue of timing is so critical to your success in your use of giving back to heal after trauma, the first question I pose may be the most important one: How much time has passed since the trauma? And is it enough for you? This isn't always a simple question to answer, so let's explore various ways to approach it.

Question 1: How much time has passed since the trauma?

One set of researchers on this issue pointed out that survivors who have continued living in war-torn areas are "not in a good position to reflect on the aftermath of trauma—for them, there is not yet an aftermath."[1] If you are still emotionally living in your own "war-torn area," you haven't yet put enough distance between you and what happened to you. In order to be helpful to others, you have to get out of the middle of your own trauma. Another study, this one of volunteers with terminal cancer patients, showed that current patients were ineffectual volunteers, because they were still coping with their own issues.[2] Those volunteers who had battled cancer and survived, on the other hand, were able to share experiences with the terminal patients they were helping. Before they could be supportive, they had to put enough distance between themselves and their own trauma.

When trauma survivors put time and energy into understanding their own experience, something interesting can happen. "Posttraumatic growth" is the process of coming out of a trauma stronger than you were before, and according to research, it isn't unusual. It appears to occur when a survivor spends time trying to make sense of what happened and in the process of reflection realizes that there were, in fact, positive outgrowths from the initially negative situation. Several studies on posttraumatic growth show survivors reporting that while they were psychologically disrupted by the trauma, they healed even beyond their pre-trauma levels.[3]

The period of reflection allows the survivor to integrate the traumatic event with his or her understanding of the world and his or her place in it. By creating something meaningful out of the challenge, a survivor often seems to emerge with a new force of will and an even better psychological status and strength than before. But taking that extra time to reflect plays a big role.

Early Stages of Recovery

How do you know if you are still in the early stages of healing and need to take a little more time before you give back to others? Here are a few of the ways you can recognize this early stage:

- Friends and family are still acting as caregivers for you on a regular basis.
- You can't get comfortable with the changes in your life.
- Your days are significantly less full than they were before your trauma.
- You wake up in the morning and have a moment where you remember your trauma, and your heart sinks.

As you get on the path to healing, it can help to recognize that the world as you know it has changed—to accept your "new normal." People around you might treat you differently. You might have a completely different day-to-day existence. You might have a new physical challenge to accommodate. Most important, you might just be seeing the world through a different lens. The world may have changed around you because of the trauma, but it could be that what changed the most is you. Your new attitude determines how you will interact with your new reality.

Integrating the new normal is often the first step in healing from trauma. But accepting the changes, both large and small, is a process that can take time. Experts suggest that keeping up your close relationships can play a key role in recovery during this first step. Supportive networks, like those we discussed in chapter 1, provide not only joy and normalcy during this critical period, but also function as a safety net that many survivors need during the dark moments. Communication with loved ones appears to aid in healing.

One thing to be aware of when you start thinking about your timing: The healing trajectory is often not a straight line. Psychological healing has both positive and negative moments along the way.

The most common example of this is when we experience "setbacks" in our healing process: We have been moving in a positive direction, healing the way we want to, and then something knocks us back. But this nonlinear reality can also show up as having happy or positive moments shortly after the initial trauma. Sometimes this can be hard for the people around us to understand. The popular concept of grief and trauma is this simple path upward—you are completely destroyed at the beginning (and therefore unable to feel any positive feelings), and then slowly the healing process sets in. People in your life who don't have an understanding of trauma might reject any divergence from that straight line, like a moment of laughter in the first darkest hours, or a day of sadness that descends on you two years later. They might tell you that what you are feeling is inappropriate. But these moments can be healthy. In his book *The Other Side of Sadness: What the New Science of Bereavement Tells Us About Life After Loss* (Basic Books, 2009), George Bonanno describes a study that showed a direct correlation between the number of times a person laughed in the first months following a spouse's death and his or her good mental health. Healing is nonlinear, so the process goes up and down each day. It is important not to judge the time it takes you to heal in a simple linear fashion.

Have you found that you've had emotions and reactions that are all over the place as you've recovered? The upside of the nonlinear nature of the healing trajectory is that even in some of the darkest moments, you still may be able to find joy. Five years after my cancer diagnosis, I went to the cancer center for a full set of scans of my whole body. The scans were just routine—no one was expecting to find any cancer. Luckily, they didn't find cancer. But they found something else.

Something almost worse.

The scans of my brain showed that I had been born with a birth defect that left the blood vessels of my brain in a tangle. For decades, I had been living with a ticking time bomb inside my head. More tests discovered that the blood vessels had indeed formed an aneurysm inside my left parietal lobe. The surgeons suggested that I immediately start the complicated process of three brain surgeries in two weeks, the last of which would be a full open craniotomy. Over the course of the three surgeries, they would remove the aneurysm from my brain completely.

During the final surgery, the neurosurgeon was going to remove a large piece of my skull in order to access my left parietal lobe. When the doctors described the surgery to me, they explained that they would be working in a spot very close to the part of my brain that controls peripheral vision and that there was a high chance that the peripheral vision on my right-hand side would be compromised. I joked with the surgical team that I was always running into door frames anyway, so no matter what they did to me they were unlikely to make matters worse. I was making jokes, yes, but they were really just to cover up my fear; it certainly wasn't a moment of joy or genuine humor. The antiseizure medicine they had put me on in preparation for the surgery had already made it hard to focus my eyes or judge distance, and going down stairs was a particular nightmare. I couldn't imagine losing any part of my vision, even just the peripheral part.

Most of all, I just wanted to wake up. My first marriage had ended, in part because of the strain of my fight with cancer, and I had only been married to my second husband for nine months when I found out I was going to need brain surgery. He hadn't signed on for this. He hadn't signed on for eight hours of pacing the waiting room to find out whether his new wife was going to live. He agreed with my decision to have the surgery, but the risks terrified him as much as they terrified me. Maybe more.

After the craniotomy, they allowed my family into the ICU to be with me while I recovered. I remember opening my eyes as the forms around me started to take shape in the dimly lit room. I could feel the squeeze of the bandages wrapped tightly around my entire head. (It sure doesn't look like it does in the movies, by the way. There's no single teensy strip of gauze. It's a giant head of nothing but bandage. Ears covered, no scalp showing—the works.) As soon as she saw my eyes flicker open, my mom reached over and put a hand on the arm that wasn't dripping with IVs. She cooed, "Sister, you're awake. You look . . ." I waited for her to admire my strength and survival and say something inspiring, like "You look amazing," or even "You look pretty good." But no. "You look . . . like a sock monkey."

She was right; I did look like a sock monkey. And the whole family cracked up—well, the rest of them laughed, and I gave a half-amused, half-in-pain snort. The ability to make a joke (at my expense) or have a good time didn't completely disappear, even in the middle of our terrifying trauma. In a 2010 Danish study, in fact, more than 50 percent of trauma survivors also experienced positive emotions and experiences after trauma, alongside the expected negative ones.[4] You may feel both joy and fear, both enjoyment and pain, while you are on the healing trajectory. The key is to know that such feelings aren't wrong or strange; they are actually a natural part of the healing process, of being who you are as you get accustomed to your new normal.

Survivors can feel the urge to participate in volunteerism too soon for many reasons: They may see giving back as a way to take action in the midst of confusion or turmoil, as a way to distract themselves, as a way to feel good in the face of pain. It may seem like the right choice to dive right in, but be aware of your motivations and of how your choice could affect you and others. If you're volunteering solely as an attempt to heal, you may not be very helpful to anyone else. And if you are volunteering to help a group of people before you've been fully healed yourself, you might even risk doing psychological harm to the intended beneficiary of your effort. It actually only takes fifteen minutes of conversation with a depressed individual for the other person to start feeling anxiety.[5] Someone who has recently suffered a trauma of their own needs you to be in strong psychological condition. If you're not, it's unlikely you will be an effective helper.

When Heidi Adams founded Planet Cancer, she did so to help young survivors get support from one another. One of the more touchy problems Heidi had at the organization was that the parents of these young cancer patients wanted to join the online support groups intended solely for young patients. Some of them had already lost their children and, in their grief, wanted to reach out to other young people. To some of the young patients they were messaging, however, it seemed as though the grieving parents were looking for stand-ins to take the place of the child they were grieving. These parents convinced themselves that they were trying to help other young people in a way they couldn't help their own child, but in nearly every case, they were unintentionally placing an emotional burden on the "replacement" child with whom they were trying to bond.

Heidi also revealed that several sets of grieving parents tried to set up foundations in memory of their children while still in the earliest stages of grief. These parents would contact Heidi within weeks or even days of their child's passing, wanting advice and partnership in creating some kind of memorial foundation or organization to honor the life of their child. In each case, the parents had a similar lack of clear vision, because they were solely driven by what their own child had needed. With time and space, these parents could have addressed widespread issues that affect a greater number of young patients in need.

While some trauma survivors try to jump in too soon, other trauma survivors who have just started their own healing process haven't yet even thought about giving back to other people—and that's completely normal. It is very common to be focused on one's own survival and reentry into the "real world" following a traumatic experience. There just might not be room in a survivor's consciousness during this phase to allow for giving back to other people. And being self-focused during the early stages can actually be incredibly healthy. Think of the phrase "charity begins at home." As a trauma survivor, you have to put your own mental, emotional, psychological, and physical health in the number-one position before you can be helpful to anyone else. Caring for yourself is an important first step.

Most people will need to regain their own footing before they start to think about offering support to others, and it's often best to start with close friends and family. It's likely that your loved ones rushed to the rescue during the initial period of crisis, offering support or taking over tasks as needed. Your journey toward giving back can begin as you reintegrate the mutual benefit that you used to have in those relationships. Both you and your inner circle might need to work hard at shifting the balance back to a shared responsibility for one another, rather than continuing the survivor-caretaker dichotomy that existed during the traumatic experience.

When you get to the later stages of the healing process, which we'll discuss in the coming chapters, you may find yourself much better prepared to take what you've learned in your own healing trajectory and apply it to helping a wider circle of other people. However, every person is different, and some people simply feel the urge to do something philanthropic for others to help them through the early stages. If that's you, I'll explore the types of opportunities you might consider toward the end of the chapter. First, let's look at questions you can ask yourself to help you make a decision that's right for you.

Deciding When the Time Is Right for You

Studies of philanthropic survivors show that giving back is a wonderful tool for healing, but that timing is a critical factor in how successful you will be. It is hard to reap the benefits of giving back that we discussed in chapter 1—like finding your purpose, regaining yourself, and making meaning of the trauma—when you're still dealing with the immediate aftermath and putting the pieces of your life back together. For most, distance and reflection are needed before those benefits come about.

So what is considered an appropriate amount of time to deal with your own crisis before reaching out to help others? Different studies on posttraumatic helping seem to suggest that between six months and two years is optimum. There is no concrete "right" time, as everyone heals differently. In fact, many nonprofits do not have regulations on when survivors can get involved with volunteering after trauma, although some larger organizations like hospitals have set a minimum requirement of one year of recovery. In many cases, however, the decision is left entirely up to the survivor. This ambiguity of what is the "right" thing to do can make it hard for survivors to make a decision, and six to twenty-four months is a big window.

In the later stages of healing, you will find that you have enough emotional distance to be a rock for those who need you and that you have the strength to act on behalf of those who have lost their strength. By following the steps in this book and answering the questions I present, you will start to see the payoff of giving back to others. But because your ability to give a part of yourself to others will grow and change dramatically the further you get along the healing trajectory, timing is critical.

The answer to the question of when to start helping depends on several factors. Consider the following questions:

- How far past does the trauma seem to you in your daily life?

- Are you back at work?

- Have you resumed your social life?

- Do you have the physical and mental stamina necessary to commit to a regular volunteer obligation?

- If you're working with a mental health professional, does that individual think you are ready to start giving back to other people?

- What type of help are you considering?

When the 2004 tsunami swept ashore at the Thai resort where model Petra Nemcova was staying with her fiancé, she had only a moment to react. She grabbed the top of a palm tree as her fiancé was swept away to sea. After hours of holding on to the tree despite her broken bones, Nemcova was rescued and taken to a hospital. She'd been critically injured, and her fiancé was killed. But despite the deep, personal effect the disaster had on her, she went back to visit Thailand just a few months later, feeling pulled to see the aftermath of the destruction and the people who, unlike her, had nowhere else to go besides their devastated homeland. There, she found wreckage where homes used to be. She saw orphaned children who had lost their entire families. Several months after the tsunami, Nemcova launched the Happy Hearts Fund, a worldwide organization that would help rebuild the lives of children affected by disasters. She used her celebrity profile to create a foundation where all administrative costs would be underwritten, so donations from individuals could be used in their entirety for direct programming expenses.

Nemcova was able to take action earlier than some people might have, in part because of the type of help she was providing: organizational, financial, awareness raising. Her process might have looked different had she chosen to devote three months to personally attending to the basic needs of orphaned children who were the victims of natural disasters. That type of work might have been too overwhelming and might have required more distance, more healing, more time.

Still, it can be easy to move too fast out of passion or a desire for healing. How can you know if you have?

Signs You May Be Moving Too Fast

Many survivors long for the resolution of the later stages of healing, so they leapfrog over important steps. How can you know if this is you? One big red flag is that you are making your volunteer experience all about yourself, rather than about the clients you're supposed to be helping.

Andy had been off the streets and working toward his GED for approximately eight months when he signed on to volunteer at a weekend retreat for individuals who had formerly been homeless. The retreat was put on by the nonprofit that had helped Andy get back on his feet, and he was considered a shining star in the program, a brilliant example of what could be accomplished when someone put his mind to rejoining society. The staff was thrilled to have him now be a volunteer.

Andy had been successful enough in his own journey that the staff members of the nonprofit were positive he'd be a great influence on the retreat attendees. He could share his story and be an inspiration to those working on accomplishing what he had already done. Instead, the opposite happened. Andy found the experience of being a leader among his peers to be cathartic, but not in an entirely helpful way. Andy couldn't stop talking about his own story all weekend, steamrolling over the stories of others. He accused those who weren't as far along on their healing trajectory of "making excuses" for why they hadn't yet accomplished the success and healing he had. He compared every experience to his own and dominated every conversation.

Andy clearly hadn't yet spent enough time recovering from his own experience of homelessness to be a true leader. Indeed, he certainly was a role model to admire from afar! He had a lot to be proud of. But he was still enmeshed enough in the traumatic experience that he wasn't able to set his own ego and desires aside and focus on the healing of other people.

Another red flag that can indicate you have moved forward too soon is a tendency to judge the experiences of others or play the comparison game in your head. Before your trauma, you may have often found yourself comparing the experiences of those around you: "She shouldn't complain that her baby doesn't sleep at night in front of Anna. Anna would give anything to just be able to get pregnant." "Joe thinks he has it bad, but at least he *has* a job." It's natural to want to play the comparison game. But that game can be dangerous when played with trauma survivors. Everyone's trauma is real and has had a deep, painful impact.

If you find yourself working as a volunteer with people and thinking, *Gosh, why are they whining? That doesn't sound so bad to me. I had it much worse when I went through that experience*, or *I don't understand why they don't just feel lucky to be alive, like I feel*, you may not have put enough distance between you and the trauma yet.

If you've found yourself in a volunteer role too early and realize you aren't yet ready, it is perfectly okay to take a step back. The staff of the nonprofit would much rather you were honest about your current abilities, I promise. No one will have hard feelings if you suggest transferring to a role more appropriate to your position on the healing trajectory (see some of the examples discussed on page 42). Don't be afraid to move around until you find the right place for you. Timing is everything, and, soon enough, you'll get to a place on your path where you can begin helping others more extensively.

Dipping Your Toes into the Philanthropic Water

John is a great example of someone who timed posttrauma giving just right. John will never forget the day *after* the day he returned home from Afghanistan. He woke up that first morning to a gray sky that felt unfamiliar following the yellow desert heat, pulled on civilian clothes he'd forgotten he owned, and confronted an unusual problem. He had nothing to do. He had nowhere to go.

For weeks, John moved through the haze of a life that felt alien to him. He was neither the same man he was before, nor could he be the soldier he had been in combat. John had to find a new job, but no one was hiring. His friends wanted to see him again, but he didn't feel connected to the group. He was different now. He hung, suspended, waiting for what his new life would look like.

While he brushed up his resume and waited for job interviews, John found himself at the local veterans center. A friend who had arrived home before him told John about the center's free counseling for returning veterans. For several months, John went to the veterans center twice a week for free services—once a week for his one-on-one sessions, and once a week for group counseling. John felt comfortable at the veterans center. As he was leaving his group session one day, many months into his participation, an employee pulled him aside.

"Do you have the next several hours free?" she asked. "Our volunteer didn't show up to work the front desk, and we need someone to answer the phones."

John didn't yet have a job—of course he had the next several hours free. And it was the first time since he'd been home that someone had asked for his help.

John happily manned the front desk that day and twice a week thereafter. He answered the phones, directed callers and visitors to the right place, and fielded questions about the work of the veterans center. He felt uniquely qualified, in fact, to direct people to the programs that help reacclimatize returning service members to their lives back home.

John's volunteer job at the veterans center is one example of how a role can be perfectly suited to someone recovering from trauma. It not only helped him along in his healing process but also allowed him to genuinely help others. John is a gatekeeper for the organization, and he is the first face many people see when visiting the site in person. Having John, who is himself a client, at the front desk might subconsciously send a message to new clients that the veterans center is a place for people just like them, a place where they can be understood.

At the same time, John's role at the front desk does not require him to have specialized knowledge of the field of posttraumatic stress disorder or veteran reentry. It is not a position where John might need the emotional distance required to hear someone else's traumatic tales from their frontline experience. John has selected a specific kind of volunteer activity that is a perfect fit for his position in the early stages of the healing trajectory.

In the first months of healing, if you have been able to come to grips with your new normal and have widened your circle of caring to encompass the people closest to you, you might start to feel eager to volunteer or take on helping roles as part of a nonprofit. Because you can't be 100 percent sure the timing is right until you have dipped your toe in the pool, you may simply have to try something to know if you're ready. But before you do, it's best to give careful consideration to the kinds of opportunities you're ready to handle at this stage.

What kinds of opportunities should you consider first, if you feel you might be ready to start giving back? Look for activities that are a one-time commitment. You want to be sure that you start slowly, especially if you haven't put a lot of time between you and the traumatic experience. Consider different ways you can test the waters. Nonprofits often have single-day volunteer activities, like stuffing envelopes or painting a house. Since you aren't making a long-term commitment, if the timing turns out to be wrong and it's a bit overwhelming to be giving back to others, you don't need to do anything other than not show up again.

—

For many survivors, coming out of the first few weeks and months of the healing trajectory can be the most disorienting. The members of your personal support system may be going about their business, heading back to their normal, pre-trauma lives. You may feel caught between two worlds: You aren't in the middle of the crisis experience anymore, yet you are not completely emotionally healed yet. You likely think about what you have been through a great deal of the time, and your experiences are still feeling very fresh in your mind.

In this stage, survivors often start to feel thankful to have made it through the time of crisis. Survivors might feel lucky to be alive, or start to feel compelled to help others in the same way they were helped. If you are just out of the beginning stages of the healing trajectory, you have started to make meaning of what has happened to you, and you might start feeling ready to give back to others. This can be a wonderful time to start getting involved with nonprofit organizations in some of the ways mentioned earlier, but we must keep this first question—how much time has passed since the trauma—in mind. The early stages of the healing trajectory are all about waiting until the time is right for you to start your philanthropy process. As we move into the questions throughout the rest of this book, however, you will probe a little deeper into how your healing process has progressed, what kind of work you put in to get where you are today, how you feel and communicate about your experiences, and what has and has not worked for you on your healing journey.

The first few months of the healing trajectory can be a critical time, as you integrate your new normal and set out on a path to recovery. If you take the time now to lay a strong foundation for healing and dip your toes in the water of giving back, you can set yourself up in a great position to give more, later. Waiting even just a few weeks or months can make a huge difference.

Be aware of the red flags, don't move too fast, and make sure your motivations are pure. Give yourself time to heal, and prepare yourself to be a rock for other people out there who will soon be relying on your strength. That time is coming!

Chapter 3

TURNING SUPPORT INTO STRENGTH

When I was first diagnosed with melanoma, I spent many days at the cancer center, getting scans and blood work, drinking barium in the CT scan lab. In all that time, I only saw one other person who seemed to be about my age. Because I felt like such an outcast among the older patients, I sought out and found Planet Cancer, the online community of young adults with cancer I introduced you to in chapter 1. At Planet Cancer, I got support from peers and could talk honestly with them about what it felt like to know that my brand-new marriage was crumbling in the middle of my melanoma diagnosis.

Through them, I found out I wasn't the only one dealing with cancer *and* marital stress. When you get cancer in your sixties or seventies, you have likely been with your partner for decades. You have made it through sleepless nights with a baby, losing a job, or cross-country moves. You have a history to fall back on. When you get cancer shortly after your first anniversary, you haven't had time to make it over any of the smaller hurdles that prepare you for the bigger ones. It helped to share my struggles with young people who were having similar experiences when it came to how cancer affected our lives. Because I had a forum in which to talk through my unique issues as a young adult with cancer, I knew my problems weren't "weird" or even very far out of the norm, and I felt less alone. Planet Cancer became my built-in base of support.

Getting the proper types of support can be a critical factor in getting and staying on the healing trajectory. By definition, trauma separates you from your life "before," and it can also separate you from the support systems you relied on previously. Your friends and family may not entirely understand what you have been through. They may feel compassion for you but also be ready for you to "shake it off" and "get back to normal." When your loved ones don't seem to understand what you need to do to heal, it can become a point of tension and can even set back your healing. Therefore, it often becomes necessary to seek out new forms of support—like what Planet Cancer was for me.

The level and type of support you receive can play an important role in how quickly you move along the healing trajectory and in how long it takes before you're ready to start volunteering. Now that we've explored how long you might need to wait before giving back to others, we're ready to ask the next two questions in our progression: Have you received any formal support? and What was the best support mechanism for you? Addressing these two questions can help you better understand how prepared you are to give back to others.

Question 2: Have you received any formal support?

For the purposes of this chapter, we'll define *formal support* as some type of professional, structured, or otherwise monitored setting, with a trained individual as the leader. Formal support can include meeting with a psychologist or a psychiatrist, attending a support group, or participating in a "matching" program with a mentor as your support system. (Informal support, on the other hand, would be friends who take you out for coffee and lend you a listening ear, for example.) Formally structured support administered via trained professionals is not an absolute necessity in healing well enough to provide service to others. But it can be a key ingredient in healing and play a vital role in helping you figure out where you are on the healing trajectory, which in turn is an integral piece of deciding if you are ready to take that final step into helping others. Whether you had a strong support network going into the trauma or not, you may also want to consider seeking out formal support.

Formal support is one way to pinpoint where you are on the healing trajectory and what issues might still be lingering. It is critically important that you are sure that you have dealt with any residual issues from your own trauma before taking on the task of helping others directly. Letting a mental health professional be a part of your healing process is one way of ensuring that you have an outsider's confirmation of your healing before you try to volunteer. A professional's opinion, while not necessary for most posttrauma volunteer roles, can be an affirmation that you are ready to go out and help others.

In addition, having some sort of professional support will give you the opportunity to watch how your counselor or support group leader helps *you*. Therefore, you will better be able to model their helping behaviors when you yourself are a role model to others, if that's the path you choose to take. In *The Seven Faces of Philanthropy*, a book on the different types of philanthropists, authors Prince and File describe one type of giver as "The Repayer," a person who has been through an event and gives back in return. These survivors, according to the authors, are "acutely aware of how others have helped them" and are motivated to repay that help.[1] Without the great support they received in the first place, these philanthropists may not have been able to give back to others as effectively as they did. But with a model of giving in mind, they were poised to "repay"—to pass it on to others.

Having a role model to show you how to help others may seem like a small thing, but by now you probably know how often people can say the "wrong" thing to trauma survivors. Being able to watch a trained individual administer support and learn from that person will hopefully keep you from putting your foot in your mouth accidentally. As you receive formal support, you will start to notice certain things that your support professional says or does that help you maximize your healing. You can then take those same tools and use them for the benefit of others.

Formal support can also be a helpful tool for discovering your own style of healing from trauma. Going through therapy or support programs teaches you a lot about yourself, the way you deal with crisis, and the way you heal. Understanding yourself in this way is going to help you on the healing trajectory (and it's going to help you answer other questions in this book, too!). Without undergoing some kind of formal support, it can take longer to access this kind of self-awareness about your healing.

Many people find participation in support groups, where the other members have experienced a similar trauma, to be a helpful way to heal. Support groups are effective because through telling the story of the traumatic incident, you actually begin to separate yourself from the moment of crisis. The traumatic experience becomes a story that you are able to tell, but over time you feel less and less inclined to relive the moment. It just becomes a part of the story of your life.

If you haven't chosen formal support for yourself, consider the reasons why. Maybe formal support just doesn't appeal to you. If you shied away from it because you felt more comfortable handling your trauma recovery by yourself, that just may be a part of your personality. That's fine, but you need to then be honest about whether you can help other people for whom that type of support *is* a part of their personality. If you aren't drawn to formal support for your own healing process, you may not get anything out of the experience of helping someone else in that way, and you need to seek out other ways of helping.

It's also possible that you've avoided formal support because you're still not comfortable sharing your story with anyone, even a trained professional. In chapter 4, I'll explore questions about telling your story and how it makes you feel. Some people also avoid formal support because they want to attempt to deal with the trauma without dealing with how they *feel* about the trauma. It can be pretty hard to do one without the other, though. If you are avoiding formal support, it could indicate that you are not as far along on the healing trajectory as you would like to be, and that perhaps you should give yourself some time before jumping into a giving-back project. Make note of your avoidance and try to understand the root causes, so you can at least be aware.

Question 3: What was the best support mechanism for you?

When you think about how you might give back to others, it is important to consider what type of support and recovery worked best for you. If you are someone who gets a lot out of sharing your emotions with others, it may not be hard for you to express your emotions to others as a way of working through them. You could be a good candidate for mentoring others and allowing them to share their emotions with you. But if you find yourself expressing your grief by taking on a new project or tearing down a wall, you have a different style of handling trauma. (We'll talk about some other implications of this in chapter 5, which explores expressing emotions.) If that is the case, you may prefer to create something or be a part of something like an event or a hands-on volunteer opportunity, where you can actually see the fruits of your labor emerge.

One way to get at the heart of this is to think deeply about the moments when you felt most comfortable during the time you were healing. It may seem like a strange thing to consider, because trauma is naturally an uncomfortable time. You probably can't use the same yardstick to measure comfort that you used before your traumatic experience. But considering your new normal, what made you feel the most at ease and secure? When did you feel supported? Was it among your friends and family? Was it with others going through the same crisis? Was it around strangers who had no idea what you were facing internally? Did you find support from other people or from information you found on the Internet? Did you find relief in church, in physical exercise, in meditation? The more closely you can identify the moments when you felt even just a little bit better, the more closely you will be able to pinpoint how you like to help others, and whether you are indeed ready to do so.

Maybe you haven't yet found the best support mechanism for yourself. Maybe you have tried a few things but haven't yet found anything that feels like it fits. You might even subconsciously be looking at volunteering or giving back to others as a cathartic experience to help yourself, because you are still on the hunt for your perfect form of support. Maybe you are thinking, *I know! Volunteering to serve others* is *my perfect form of support!* But remember, as we discussed in chapter 2, that it's usually not best to help others as a way of working through your own trauma. It can easily backfire. If you haven't yet found your perfect support mechanism, keep looking.

Identifying the best support mechanism for you will help you as you seek out ways to find meaning in giving back. Reflecting heavily on your various support experiences, both the successes and the challenges, before moving on to help others can also serve as a springboard for looking at whether you have the ability to separate your own experiences and struggles from those of the people you will want to help.

As you know by now, if you move into giving back to others without first having built a solid foundation of support for yourself, you may find you are unprepared to give the support to others that is expected of you. Challenge yourself to make sure you have started putting the emotional and psychological framework in place that will give you the strength you need as a philanthropist. Spend some time reflecting on the support you have received and the ways it has helped you, so you can know your own abilities and limitations when it comes to giving back to others.

Considering the Type of Support You Might Offer

Choosing the right volunteer activity for you—based on an analysis of what methods of giving and receiving support you're comfortable with—is just as important as waiting an appropriate amount of time before leaping into helping roles. Many people choose to support others in a way that's related to their own trauma, or in a way that someone supported them, but even within each single cause there are many different ways to help. You could choose to mentor someone on a weekly basis or bring care packages to a hospital. You could work on a fundraising event or build a website. The list goes on. By thinking about your own experience of receiving support, you can choose an option that fits best for you.

Lara was a survivor of a childhood seizure disorder similar to epilepsy. She remembers having a seizure during a junior high school social studies class and being referred to for the next six years as the Girl Whose Eyes Rolled Back in Her Head. During her summer breaks, from sixth grade through tenth grade, Lara attended a summer camp for children with seizure disorders. At camp, finally, Lara wasn't a weirdo. She wasn't that strange kid who had to keep going to the nurse's office during fourth period. Everyone at camp was just like her. Lara made her two dearest friendships with other girls at camp, because her new friends understood. These friendships lasted into adulthood, as the three women supported each other in their health struggles and all of the other struggles that come with growing up.

Lara became a successful adult, finishing law school and joining a prestigious practice. A local nonprofit providing support services, medical information, and grants to people living with seizure disorders was thrilled to be introduced to a rising young star like Lara. Because she was an attorney, the organization drafted Lara onto the board of directors and asked her to play a key role in writing policy for the organization and helping them lobby for better healthcare legislation for the epilepsy and seizure disorder population.

Lara was happy to help out, and she liked being a part of something so important to her. But at the same time, she didn't feel like she was doing what she was most passionate about. She really wanted to work with teenagers just like the friends she met at camp, who were dealing with a medical issue that could cause them to be an outcast at an already critical point in their lives. What Lara wanted more than writing policy was to really work with the teenagers and help them cope with the difficulties of being different because of their medical condition.

It's understandable that the organization wanted Lara on its board of directors. She possessed not only an understanding of the issues, from having lived through them, but also a specialized skill set that many nonprofit boards look for. Often, nonprofits will ask you to take on a specific role that dovetails with your profession. Maybe that appeals to you. But some people think, *I've been doing that all day, every day. When I volunteer and give back, I want to do something different from my day job.* If you don't fully understand what type of support you want to offer, you run the risk of getting drafted into something that isn't a good fit.

Lara finally realized what was nagging at her about her participation with the nonprofit. It wasn't, of course, that she didn't believe in the mission; it was that, for her, the most helpful moments in getting through her childhood health struggles had been the peer support and social opportunities with other people like her. Helping in that way was what was going to be meaningful to her, not board service. When Lara finally realized that she could give back in a way that mirrored her own most successful healing path, she became a camp counselor for two weeks every summer, working with the teenagers in addition to her board position. Her new role helped Lara recommit to her work with the organization, and she finally felt fulfilled.

The question of which support systems worked best for you will help you understand what form of support really speaks to you, so that—like Lara—you can end up making a smart choice. If you preferred group support networks, seek out organizations that provide similar activities. If you preferred working one-on-one with a mentor, then you can sign up to be matched with someone newly facing the same trauma you have already survived.

Gathering the Emotional Strength to Give Back

The answer to the question of whether you have the emotional foundation to start giving back to others is unique to you, and it depends on several factors. Consider the following:

- In what ways have I been able to use the support systems available to me in order to deal with my emotions?

- If I have not used formal support systems, why not?

- Are there support systems out there that I know won't work for me? Why do I feel that they won't work?
- What does my support team think I am emotionally prepared for, in terms of giving back to others?

If you have a formal support system you've been relying on to get through your trauma-healing process, you likely have some great clues as to what you might be ready for, and you hopefully have some mentors you can discuss your options with. But even if you are still in the middle of receiving therapy or working with a support group, there are options for you to start giving back at a level that won't disrupt your own emotional process.

A perfect way to engage with nonprofits in a way that isn't too emotionally risky is by helping in a behind-the-scenes capacity. Nonprofit organizations don't always advertise or discuss their behind-the-scenes volunteer opportunities up front, but most nonprofits have needs in this area. Behind-the-scenes volunteer tasks include things like answering the phones for new clients and preparing end-of-the-year reports to mail out to donors. These tasks are critical to the mission of the nonprofit, and someone has to do them, but often nonprofits can't afford to pay someone to fill this role. By taking on a behind-the-scenes volunteer job with a nonprofit, you are helping the organization continue to operate while allowing more money to go toward the programs.

Volunteering to do these behind-the-scenes tasks while you are still working through the emotional progression of your healing trajectory can also be a great way to set the stage for more comprehensive involvement to come. Because you are building a relationship with a nonprofit as you work behind the scenes for them, you are learning important details about their operations and about other ways you can help later. You will be able to look at all their program offerings, the way they operate, and the future volunteer roles available to you, and make smart decisions about what other ways you might help the organization as you move along in your healing process.

One activity many middle-stage survivors get involved with is nonprofit events. Most nonprofit organizations have a schedule of different events and activities throughout the year. These events are intended to raise money for the organization at the same time that they raise community awareness about the nonprofit's mission and the issues they are working to solve. Events are a great way for a nonprofit to interact with the community and bring more people into its network—and a great way for you to get involved without making a long-term or recurring commitment.

Nonprofit activities can take several forms. One of the most common is an organized walk, run, or other physical activity. Usually money is raised through participant entry fees, or participants are asked to raise money through getting pledges from the people in their network. As a volunteer, you could participate as a walker or a runner (or a swimmer, a biker, a hiker—whatever!). You could also choose to volunteer on the day of the event as support staff. If you choose to work at an event for a nonprofit in an area related to your own trauma experience, you might find that the event has a special role for survivors, like handing out goodies at the finish line.

Another type of nonprofit activity is a gala or party. These more formal events are typically cocktail parties or seated dinners, and the money is raised through tickets or tables sold, as well as through small activities like live auctions or silent auctions during the evening. As a volunteer, you might work check-in, take pictures of attendees, or help work the auction tables.

In your community, you may also find many other types of

unique nonprofit events besides athletic events or galas. There may be concerts for a cause, or poetry contests where money is raised for a nonprofit organization—the list is endless. One benefit of giving back through events is that not only can you match the cause to something you care about, but you can also hopefully find an activity that you enjoy as an individual, not just as a survivor. If you like to dress up and go out, you're the perfect candidate to volunteer at a gala. If you are an athlete, there's bound to be a nonprofit athletic event that is right up your alley. Nonprofit events require a lot of human capital to plan and execute (not to mention to clean up after!), so there is always a great need for volunteers.

—

If you're still working on the emotional lessons of the healing trajectory, if you're still working through the formal support process, some of the volunteer opportunities just mentioned are the perfect place for you to give back now. If you have not received formal support, either in a group environment or in one-on-one meetings with a professional, you might not be a strong candidate to volunteer as an emotional support system for someone else just yet. You will be unfamiliar with the more formal processes and strategies to reach healing, which will make it difficult for you to relate. You might not have internalized the steps the people you are helping will be going through. In their training, even professional therapists are required to see a therapist for a period of time. There's a reason for that requirement: It's good to practice what you preach.

Don't worry if you don't yet feel prepared for some of the activities in this chapter. You can always stick with the volunteer activities described in chapter 2 for as long as you need. Or, heck, forever, if that's what you prefer! The whole point of this chapter is beginning to understand what works for you and what doesn't. You'll work on understanding your own relationship with giving back even more in the coming chapters. The key is to work through this and figure out what's best for you, so that you can give your best to someone else. Once you have spent time getting the formal support *you* need and understanding the ways it has worked to heal you, you can start to move forward into applying that help to other people.

Chapter 4

TELLING YOUR STORY—OR NOT

"Oh my gosh, you should write a book!"

That's what many people tell trauma survivors when they hear our stories of crisis and endurance. There's something about a good survival story that has everyone rooting for us and wanting to hear yet again the tale that makes them gasp, shake their heads, and feel glad they aren't in our shoes.

Dealing with the story of your trauma—and how you share it with others—emerges as a key issue as your healing progresses. People around you will want to talk about what happened to you. You will likely be asked questions by concerned friends, or by your colleagues if you go back to work. At first, you may not feel like talking about what you've been through, which is perfectly normal. It can be hard enough at times just to live it, let alone talk about it with people who don't necessarily understand. But as time goes on, you may grow to feel more comfortable telling the story of your trauma. And that's a good thing! Your ability and willingness to talk about your experience can be a great barometer to test when you will be ready to help others, and what methods of giving back will be best suited to you.

When you talk about what happened to you, you can inspire or educate other people, either people who are going through what you have been through or people who have no idea but want to learn. Using your story to help others can be a very valuable way of giving back, but it requires caution. As mentioned in chapter 2, a study that looked at interactions with depressed people showed that within fifteen minutes of conversation, a nondepressed individual who was talking to a depressed individual would begin to feel increased anxiety and depression, as well as hostility toward the depressed person they were talking to.[1] If you aren't ready to tell your story, it won't do the listener any good.

If you are ready to tell your story, though, sharing your experience can be almost medicinal, for the other person and especially for you. As I mentioned in chapter 3 in the context of group support, telling your story not only helps you internalize and "own" it, but it can also put it in perspective for you. When you tell your story of trauma and hear someone else's in return, you get the opportunity to change your point of view on what you have been through.

One young gentleman I met has a name for this phenomenon—he calls it the "sucks to be you" syndrome. Steven told me a story about how, as a young man with cancer, he was introduced to Heidi, the founder of Planet Cancer, whom I first introduced you to in chapter 2. Steven and Heidi traded tales about their hairless chemotherapy days and overly protective parents. He explained to her what he had gone through to beat his brain tumor, and she regaled him with tales of going through bone cancer. While listening to her story, Steven recalls thinking, *Man! That sucks. I'm so glad I didn't have to go through that.* It wasn't until their friendship had grown over several years that one day Steven shared that story with Heidi, admitting he had felt bad for her. Imagine his surprise when she responded, "You felt bad for *me*? I listened to what you went through and I was thinking that it sucked to be *you*!"

Both Steven and Heidi had adapted to their own situation to the point that they had accepted it and therefore felt that it wasn't nearly as bad as what others were going through. Hearing a friend's story and telling their own made them, if not grateful for what had happened to them, at least grateful it wasn't worse. "Sucks to be you" syndrome is about the perspective that the devil you know beats the devil you don't. You have already been through your challenge, and you emerge with the perspective that you were capable of handling it.

Sharing your story when you are ready can hold great benefits, but you have to be ready to put it in perspective. When you can do that, it's a sign that you may be ready to give back in other ways and that telling your story can be beneficial to you and others. So, carefully consider the two questions in this chapter—Are you able to tell the story of what happened? and How do you feel when talking about the trauma?—as you develop plans to begin giving back.

Question 4: Are you able to tell the story of what happened?

The ability to tell the story is an important stepping-stone on the healing trajectory. If you can talk to other people about your crisis without the memories being too painful or overwhelming, then you have successfully integrated the trauma into your life's narrative and accomplished some level of emotional healing.

In many ways, verbalizing what happened to you can actually move the healing process along. As with so many things survivors face after trauma, the more you do it, the easier and more natural it becomes. Because coming to grips with your new normal is so important, the more you tell your story, the more real your new normal becomes to you. Telling your story is a concrete way of accepting and embracing a transformed reality.

The way you deal with telling your story can also reveal other things about how you are handling the healing process. One study of posttraumatic coping found that the survivors who exhibited the best coping skills were the ones who could either share or not share their traumatic experiences, depending on what the situation called for.[2] Being comfortable with your story does *not* necessarily mean sharing your story with anyone, anywhere. Have you run across someone in your healing process who does that—who talks to nearly anyone and everyone about what happened to them? Those people share *all* the gory details, probably more than the listener wants to hear, and they don't even seem to notice the discomfort of the person listening to this intimate tale. This sharing—which can happen in line at the grocery store and on the treadmills at the gym—can really be *over*sharing, and it often isn't the healthiest way to get comfortable with telling your story. The survivors who are the most healed have the ability to tell the story of their trauma when appropriate, but they also have the ability to hold back if the situation calls for it. It is important to have integrated your story enough that you are able to share it, but also to have reached enough healing that your trauma isn't the only thing you can focus on in conversation.

We've already discussed how important it can be to realize that everyone's healing trajectory is different. One of the reasons for this is that everyone's personality is different. Your comfort level, and not just your level of healing, plays a huge role when you tackle this particular issue. Talking about your trauma may not be your preferred coping method. Verbally telling your story, either to one person or to a group, may not be a tool that actually helps you achieve healing. That may just naturally be who you are. Even if telling the story isn't a healing tactic for you, however, it is still something that will be required of most survivors at one point or another. And if you serve as a role model and leader for other people who are going through trauma, there is a very high likelihood that you will be asked to talk about your experience. It can be important, if you want to work with other individuals who are still in the middle of their crisis, that you work on acclimating to your new normal and telling your story comfortably, appropriately, and confidently.

Question 5: How do you feel when talking about the trauma?

The ability to tell the story is one important factor in determining how far along on the healing trajectory you are. It also helps to spend time thinking about how you *feel* when you talk about your traumatic experience. Do you feel drained? Do you feel annoyed at the intrusion? Do you feel energized?

In some cases, your emotional reaction to recounting your experience can be simply a factor of time. You may find that the more time you put behind you, the easier it is for you to tell the story without feeling emotionally drained or distraught. For some people, the more they retell their story over time, the less of an emotional grip it has. Your feelings may absolutely change as time goes on. But at some point, your feelings about the story will become fairly consistent, and that moment is a great time to evaluate your reactions to the story of your trauma.

Not every survivor wants to tell and retell the story of his or her trauma over and over again as part of the volunteer experience. If you feel depressed or drained from telling your story, or if it causes you to relive any of your past feelings—like helplessness—you should reconsider serving in this way. It may not end up being satisfying to you or beneficial to the listeners. There are so many other ways to give back that will fit your needs and your style.

A common struggle survivors face as they begin telling the story of their trauma is dealing with other people's responses and misinterpretations. Take, for example, how listeners sometimes misunderstand the language of survivors. It's not uncommon for survivors to express feeling "lucky" or appreciative of certain aspects of their experiences. It has become common to hear trauma survivors say, "In hindsight, I am grateful for the accident/illness/trauma experience, because I now appreciate things more." People who listened to me tell my story, for example, would have heard me say, "I am so lucky" and that "Cancer saved my life" because I found the aneurysm. Sometimes people who heard me express those feelings misunderstood, believing that those emotions meant I had completed the psychological process of healing.

As a survivor, you can't fault outsiders for misinterpreting. But these are complex emotions indicative of a point on the healing trajectory. Making meaning of the trauma and understanding some of the benefits of the experience is just a part of the process. As you are telling your story to the outside world, you are likely to come across misunderstandings of this sort. People who have not been through trauma may not have the same depth of understanding or be familiar with the vocabulary survivors often use to describe their experiences or emotions. Telling your story comfortably may mean that you need to be prepared for this kind of misinterpretation, and you may need to be explicit when explaining to people what you mean when you tell your story of psychological healing.

Another phenomenon that can impact how a survivor feels about telling his or her story is survivor's guilt—thoughts like *Why did I survive when so many other people haven't? I don't deserve to live any more than they did.* Survivor's guilt is most common among trauma survivors who have faced combat service, life in a war-torn region, or life-threatening illnesses like cancer. Survivor's guilt can often happen long before a person volunteers. The death of a friend, colleague, fellow service member, or even acquaintance from the chemo infusion room can trigger feelings of guilt: You survived while the other person's loved ones must grieve. These guilty feelings can become even more pronounced when you are in a position of leadership as a volunteer and one of your clients has a bad outcome. Volunteers in this position sometimes say they felt a sense of responsibility, like they should have "done more" for their clients, who look to them to prevent further suffering. Survivor's guilt plays off of the unfairness and sometimes the unpredictability of trauma situations, and when you're feeling it, it's hard to tell your story in a way that supports both you and the hearer.

In this way, survivor's guilt can inhibit your ability to be a strong volunteer. The clients you help—even those who are struggling most—do not need your pity. They need your strength. It is important for you to cope with your own feelings of survivor's guilt, if you have experienced them, before you attempt to work with others in crisis. Even if you have never experienced survivor's guilt before, think about what you would do if confronted by someone in a significantly worse situation than your own. You have to be prepared to work through the guilt that might come with that relationship. By telegraphing guilt, you may be unintentionally sending the message that you are glad not to be in their position. Someone deep in crisis should not be burdened with the negative emotions of the very people who are supposed to be there to support them.

Choosing Whether to Leverage Your Experience

Choosing the right type of philanthropy is especially important when it comes to choosing the roles in which you will be called upon to tell your story. Advocacy, for example, is a volunteer role where survivors may make informational presentations about their experience. Those volunteer advocates who are emotionally healed and who also like to share their story report feeling positive after their presentations, like they have done something worthwhile to effect change. Volunteer advocates who are not fully prepared for this type of participation, however, often find that speaking out leaves them drained and unsatisfied.

I saw this firsthand one afternoon when I went with a group of young adult cancer survivors to speak to the fourth-year medical students at a nearby university. These medical students, though not much older than we were ourselves, would soon be doctors on the front lines. Soon, they would be faced with patients just like us. We had a moment to tell them, as both peers and patients, what it felt like to be on the receiving end of a diagnosis. Over the years, many of the young medical students have reported that watching our panel speak changed the way they related to young adults with cancer once they became physicians themselves.

One year, though, a panel member named Tara got choked up when retelling the story of her surprising diagnosis. Her diagnosis had indeed been a traumatic experience, and she was hoping that by participating on the panel, she could teach young doctors not to treat their patients as thoughtlessly as the doctors in the emergency room had treated her. As Tara tells it, she was all alone, off at college, and it was the middle of the night. The doctors, indifferent to the fear of such a young woman, broke the news at two o'clock in the morning while she sat all alone. They told her, "The tests came back; it's cancer," and then left the room immediately. She couldn't reach her parents by phone to share the news.

Tara could barely finish the story. Though the audience was moved by her experience, she was quiet and dejected the rest of the day, picking at what should have been a celebratory lunch. On the other hand, I felt elated after the panel. I had just used my story to keep new patients from having to deal with doctors who didn't understand the enormity of delivering bad news. I was several years further along the healing trajectory than Tara, and I was more prepared than she to tell my story in a way that made me feel empowered. The same experience affected the two of us in different ways, because we had been through different healing processes and experiences along the way. I was prepared and eager to speak my feelings out loud, while Tara didn't really benefit in a positive way from the experience.

Some survivors eventually feel ready to take up a highly committed role: that of advocate and activist. If telling your story is an energizing and motivating experience for you, then you may be ideally suited to a role such as this. Every cause needs the voices of survivors who are willing to speak up and serve as advocates. As a survivor yourself, you are in an ideal position to use your story to draw attention to the cause. You could be an advocate, an activist, or a lobbyist. You could give media interviews on behalf of an organization, or serve as the keynote speaker at a fundraising event. Before taking on these visible, outspoken roles, however, spend some time figuring out the answer to the questions in this chapter.

Sometimes, the choice about whether to be open about your story isn't entirely up to you. If your trauma caused a visible injury or change in your ability—if you lost your hair to chemo, for example—people may come right up and ask. In the case of Jerry, whom you met in chapter 1, people were often unable to contain their curiosity about a man who was obviously physically fit yet confined to a wheelchair. Jerry had to create some kind of response, even in the moments when he didn't really feel like talking about it. What he discovered, though, can also be a tool for you: The things you say about your story can and will change as time goes on. At first, you might need to come up with a short, canned response that feels safe and isn't too much of an emotional trigger for you, something like "I was in an accident. Thanks for understanding." As time goes on and you practice telling the story of your trauma, it is natural that your comfort level will increase, and you can add the details that feel natural to you. If you notice those adaptations to your story—the growing content and addition of more intimate details—it might be an indicator that you are more ready to share your story as a volunteer and to start working with clients or other people who need to hear what you have been through.

You may, however, be someone who, no matter how progressed your healing is, will never get excited about telling your story. A mentor once pointed out to me the difference between "personal" and "private." Sharing things that feel personal to us can be a revelatory experience for other people. But we are always in control of what we share, and we always have the power to keep the private stuff private. Where you draw the line between personal and private is up to you. If you feel like you could share your story but just don't want to, that's entirely okay, and it's a great thing for you to realize about yourself. Or maybe you don't mind if your story gets told in order to help other people, but you don't necessarily want to be the one who stands up at the lectern and tells it. In that case, a nonprofit could use your story on its website or in promotional materials to draw attention to the cause. You don't always have to be the teller of your story. There are ways your story can still be leveraged, if you so choose.

Christopher Reeve is an extraordinary example of someone who used his story to move communities to action. But then again, who expects Superman to be ordinary? As an actor and director, Reeve was a professional success. As a husband and father, he was loved and content. When Reeve fell off his horse during an equestrian competition in 1995, his spinal cord was irreparably damaged.

Reeve instantly went from superhero to quadriplegic. He could not walk, stand, or breathe on his own.

Reeve and his wife Dana sprung to action. Reeve visited Israel, where spinal cord research was surpassing what was being done in the United States. The couple made large donations to the Reeve-Irvine Research Center and founded the Christopher and Dana Reeve Foundation, which has given tens of millions of dollars in research grants to date. In addition to his own significant financial gifts, Reeve also helped raise money for research and quality-of-life issues, to promote longer, better lives for spinal cord injury patients.

Michael J. Fox, like Christopher Reeve, was already a household name when tragedy struck. At age thirty, he was diagnosed with Parkinson's disease. In his first book, *Lucky Man*, Fox reveals that he was in denial of his own diagnosis for the first seven years. Though it took him years to accept the illness and disclose his diagnosis to the public, he ultimately founded the Michael J. Fox Foundation for Parkinson's Research. The foundation focuses on research and clinical trials that provide promising avenues for treatments and, eventually, a cure. Fox is a founder, an advocate, a donor, and the face of the organization.

The role of outspoken advocate usually requires not just that time has passed and healing is well under way but also that the survivor has a skill set that is well suited for the job. Advocates have the ability to take their story of survival and use it to inspire others to make some kind of desired change. This might mean an increase in funding, a change in legislation, or simply an upsurge in awareness. The role of an advocate can be a critical one that brings aid to a cause; having a leader step forward to serve as the face of an issue can be the difference between people embracing the issue or having it fade away into obscurity.

If you choose to serve as an advocate or activist, you may be required to volunteer at odd times and in unexpected ways. You might receive a call at midnight to appear on a morning television show at 6:00 a.m. that very day. You might need to travel to remote locations to speak up for your cause to a critical audience. Because you are using your story to be a public figure for the cause, you will also need to take special care in how you present yourself. Some volunteer advocates receive media training, where they learn to respond appropriately and watch their language and image very carefully in interviews. Some advocates, because they have become such a visible leader for their cause, find that they need to pay attention to how they comport themselves even when they are "off duty."

Survivors who seek to take on the role of advocate should be prepared to speak publicly, to retell their story over and over, and even to handle criticism. Indeed, for every issue, there is someone else on the other side who disagrees, or someone who thinks funding and focus should go to a different issue. A survivor who steps forward as the face of an awareness campaign runs the risk of drawing negative attention as well as positive. In "real life," most survivors receive compassion and sometimes even deference, so it can be a cruel shock for an unprepared survivor who takes on the role of advocate to find him- or herself being publicly judged. Despite the difficulties, becoming an advocate for a cause you care about can be one of the more meaningful volunteer roles for a survivor. Advocacy is a role in which your story can have a wider impact than you may have ever expected.

The answer to the question of whether you're ready to start telling your story as a part of the way you give back to others depends on several factors. Consider the following questions:

- Have I practiced telling my story out loud to a support professional, a support group, or even my friends and family?

- If I haven't, why not?

- When a stranger asks me questions about my experience, how do I perceive that person? Do I feel like they are nosy? Do I resent the intrusion? Or do I relish the chance to educate them?

- What parts of my story do I think other people might be able to learn from or be inspired by?

- If I imagine sharing my story with a room full of five hundred people, would I feel like I had accomplished something afterward? Or in my mind's eye, did I choke up with emotion and have to stop before I finished?

Telling our stories has an amazing ability to bring healing and perspective to those around us, and even to ourselves. When we hear about someone else's challenge, our own challenge doesn't seem so large anymore. A leadership trainer I look up to told me about a trick she uses to help the groups she coaches get perspective. She asks everyone to write on a piece of paper the biggest challenge they face right now. The challenges her audiences write down, she says, range from work challenges to family challenges, relationship challenges to health challenges. Then she invites everyone to come up to the whiteboard and write their challenge. After all the challenges are up on the board, she asks everyone to take a look at what all of their colleagues are facing. "What do you feel when looking up at the board?" she asks them. "When you were just looking at your own challenge, it seemed like the biggest challenge in the world to you, didn't it? How many of you would like to walk back up there and erase your challenge, now that you see it up there next to everyone else's?"

It is not that life challenges are a comparison game. It doesn't matter deep inside what anyone else is going through or how it compares, because a person's challenges are big to them, or else they wouldn't be challenges. When you tell your story, in whatever way is comfortable for you, you are shifting the listener's perspective on the challenges of life. Whether you tell your story to the world, write it on a website, or share it with only your closest family members, you give others the chance to shift their frame of mind and put the gifts they do have into perspective. Sharing your story and hearing the stories of others can be a great way to give the world a perspective shift. No matter who is listening, your story can make a difference.

Chapter 5

ΕXPRESSING YOUR EMOTIONS—OR NOT

When you go through a trauma, you often aren't in control. You can lose control over your health, your finances, your life circumstances, or your ability to take on tasks that used to be simple. What's another one of the most common things to lose control over when it comes to a crisis situation? Your emotions. Though your emotions "belong" to you, in a sense you don't control them. That's never more obvious than when you are in a trauma or trauma-healing situation. In those times, you can often feel like you belong to your emotions, like they have the control over you.

One of the important elements of the healing trajectory is coming to grips with your emotions: Understand exactly what they are, how healthy they are, how they are driving you, and how you can regain control of them. Your emotional state and how you express your emotions will impact your decisions about how and when to help others. As with so many other parts of the healing process, understanding our emotions and how they affect our decisions can be very personal, and everyone deals with their emotions in different ways.

When I went through my brain aneurysm, I already wore the title of Survivor. I had beaten cancer (twice, no less—I'd had a second, minor bout with melanoma three years after the first). I knew what it felt like to make decisions in the face of overwhelming fear and to struggle through recovery to the other side. You could say that no one was more prepared than I was for the three brain surgeries that were to come. And it showed. When I was originally diagnosed, I handled the news calmly and scientifically. By the evening of the day I got the news, I had already identified my top choice in neurosurgeons, if indeed he agreed surgery was necessary. I had arranged for copies of my scans to be sent to the different surgeons I was going to interview. I had started making a list of the pros and cons of surgery versus other, nonsurgical treatment options. My matter-of-fact attitude carried me right through the surgery, and I made logical, educated decisions along the way. I knew what questions to ask after I woke up. I knew to expect the long, painful recovery that I experienced (although no amount of knowledge could *quite* prepare me for that).

There was only one thing I didn't do very well. Too bad it was one of the more important things. I didn't take a moment to really let my emotions sink in. Having been through a health trauma before, I just plowed right on forward with an attitude of "Here we go again. I've got this under control." It took me an entire year to realize what I had done. Late one February night, a year to the week after my first set of tests, I was walking with my husband. We were on vacation in beautiful Santa Fe and were walking back to our hotel after dining out. We navigated the sandy, bumpy, sidewalk-less roads in a historic neighborhood, where you can look up and actually see stars. I said, "I just can't believe it was a year ago. I can't believe that a year ago I was checking into the hospital for the first time." It didn't seem like it could have been so far away. I kept asking him to relive certain parts of the experience with me. "Do you remember when I woke up? How much pain I was in? Do you remember making me walk around the kitchen that first day we got home, and I couldn't do it? Do you remember how scared I got the first time I tried to read, and I couldn't?"

Finally he turned to me and said, "You have really been asking a lot of these questions the past few weeks. You seem more scared now, after it's all over, than you did during the whole process. Why are you still so worked up over these moments? You're past them now." It was as though a lightbulb went on, and the stars above me blurred as I got tears in my eyes.

"I think I wasn't really as strong as I was acting, back then," I confessed. As the words came out of my mouth, I knew they were the truth. At the time, I had stayed strong to give hope to the people around me and to take away some of their fear. And probably to deny my own fear. It turns out, none of it worked. Your emotions usually come out, one way or another, at one time or another. By acknowledging them and understanding them, you can rob them of their power to control you without your knowledge.

The questions in this chapter—Do you still live in fear that something terrible may happen? and How do you express grief and stress in general?—are designed to help you think through emotions that often linger after a trauma, and to help you come to grips with them so you're prepared to support others in need. You will also get a chance to honestly assess the best way you, individually, deal with your emotions, because we're all different.

Question 6: Do you still live in fear that something terrible may happen?

You have probably heard the story of Chicken Little. Chicken Little (or Henny Penny, in some versions of the tale) thought the sky was falling and ran around telling all her barnyard friends that the end of the world was upon them. She spent her days hysterical, looking up at the sky, waiting for what she perceived to be imminent doom. For Chicken Little, the sky was definitely going to fall; she just didn't know exactly when it was going to happen. As trauma survivors, we've already had the sky fall on us once. So who can blame us if we feel a little bit like Chicken Little, always waiting for those clouds to open up and the sky to start raining down on us yet again?

It is not uncommon for survivors to be left with a nagging sense that there is still something terrible yet to happen in the future—that the worst isn't over yet. If your trauma was illness-related, this anxiety often centers on thoughts about the disease coming back or flaring up again. If your trauma is related to the loss of a loved one, you might panic every time someone you love seems to be at the slightest risk of a health problem. If your trauma is related to an accident, you might get emotionally triggered by watching the news or reading the newspaper.

It's perfectly normal to experience a feeling of holding your breath and waiting for the other shoe to drop after you have survived a major life challenge. Once your life is completely changed by trauma, your survival instincts kick in and you start to believe that if the worst was possible before, anything is possible now. And if you are so caught up in the aftermath of your own trauma that you think you are still in danger, you won't able to focus on the suffering of others. Eventually, once you're further along the healing trajectory, you realize that danger and loss are no longer lurking around every corner; you'll gain control of your fear. And if you want to give back to others, especially if you're going to work directly with other people, it helps to get to a place where you aren't waiting for the bottom to drop out of your life again.

This positive outlook, that the worst is behind you and that you're ready to move forward, is often inversely related to how helpless you felt during the initial trauma and how helpless you continue to feel. Researchers who study posttraumatic growth (that phenomenon we touched on in chapter 2, where positive psychological changes follow a trauma—very much the opposite of posttraumatic stress disorder) noted that survivors have to be able to move on psychologically from the trauma in order to experience that positivity.[1] One of the goals of giving back to other people is providing you with a set of positive actions you can take that will improve lives, including your own.

The healing trajectory holds promise for trauma survivors. At some point, the daily fear and pain will be over. In many cases, people who have gone through trauma can have even richer and fuller lives afterward than they did before. Research psychologist and the father of positive psychology Martin Seligman administered a test to 1,700 participants and found that survivors of trauma had higher well-being scores than individuals who had not experienced trauma, and that the more trauma a survivor had experienced, the stronger his or her well-being score was.[2] The trauma survivors were happier and felt more positive promise in life than people who had never been challenged. In fact, people who had experienced two or more traumas saw their well-being scores go up even *more*!

We hear over and over that challenge can make someone a better person. "Cancer is a gift." "I'm glad it happened; I'm a better person now." Phrases like that are bitter pills to swallow while you're in the middle of a trauma. But the outcome Seligman found supports their validity: With the proper healing, you can be one of those people whose outlook is better after trauma than it was before.

It seems impossible, doesn't it? How could you be positive after everything you've been through? How could you not spend the rest of your life waiting for catastrophe? But the scientific evidence is clear. You don't have to. If you do the hard work of healing, you are more prepared to join the ranks of people who have a better outlook when they make it to the other side. Keep in mind that there isn't a shortcut to getting to that point. The path is different for everyone. But there is a common need to work through the elements of healing and to get from feeling like you will never be whole again to realizing you are, in fact, a different person but still just as complete as you were before.

Regardless of where you started or where you end up, you will eventually cease waiting for the sky to fall down like Chicken Little did. You won't expect bad news every time the phone rings. That light at the end of the tunnel is coming, and when it does, you'll be ready to devote even more of yourself to volunteering and giving back.

Question 7: How do you express grief and stress in general?

As I've said repeatedly, there is no one single way to heal. If you are holding on to the notion that your own healing process has to look a certain way, let it go. If you are comparing your healing trajectory to that of others, or allowing other people to do so, you're doing yourself a disservice. Just as people let go of the fear of a second trauma at different stages, they also express the emotions of grief and stress in different ways.

Grief expert Kenneth Doka wondered if men and women express grief differently from one another, in much the way they seem to express feelings in general differently. His findings indicated that there isn't necessarily a distinction that runs cleanly along gender lines, but that there are nevertheless two distinct grieving styles.[3] Women, on the whole, are more likely to exhibit what is called the "intuitive grieving" style. In that behavior pattern, the survivor's experience is all about the expression of emotions. Often, intuitive grieving patterns are more obvious to the outside world, closer to what we most commonly recognize as grief.

The "instrumental grieving" style, on the other hand, appears more often but not exclusively in men. Instrumental grief relies on processing the grief physically, through outward actions. Though the grief is not communicated verbally or through emotional expressions such as tears, the survivor is still grieving. The instrumental griever may find solace in taking up a sport, in gardening, or in building something.

Your emotional style plays a big role in how you decide to give back to others. Consider the following questions as you explore your emotional style:

- Are you a person who prefers to "get it all out"? Or are you still waters that run deep?

- How do you handle regular annoyances and challenges in everyday life? (We can often see reflections of how we will deal with life's major traumas and respond to the traumas of others when we look at our day-to-day activities.)

- Are you unable to move forward mentally until you've solved a problem? Or do you like to walk away and put some distance between yourself and the issue at hand? Do you like to entertain yourself and forget about it for a little while before coming back to it?

Let's be clear about different emotional styles: Not wanting to express your emotions doesn't necessarily equate to not being *comfortable* with your emotions. Just because you don't always speak from an emotional space doesn't mean you don't *have* emotions, and it doesn't even necessarily mean you aren't in touch with them. It just means you may not be on a first-name basis with them, like other people may be with theirs. Reluctance to ever share your emotions can perhaps but not necessarily be an indicator that you have some uncomfortable feelings lurking deep down. But it may just be your style. If this is the case, it's best to know before going into a volunteering opportunity. For example, if you aren't someone who communicates your emotions, you might not have the patience to listen to those who do. So, when you spend time finding volunteer and philanthropic opportunities, look for ones that fit your emotional style.

When it comes to working through the residual grief and stress of your trauma, the important part is not what you choose to do, but that you do it at all. As long as you're addressing it, you are on the right track. But do take note of your emotional style, because your preferences will indicate what volunteer roles you will be more drawn to.

Finding the Right Level of Emotional Engagement

Until you can feel optimistic that the worst is over and have worked through the worst of your grief and stress, you might want to limit your volunteering to indirect activities. Face-to-face volunteering like mentoring might bring up memories or issues you're still working on. As a direct-service volunteer, some of the people you work with might have been through a similar trauma and might even have had a worse outcome. You might not be able to emotionally separate yourself from their prognosis, their outlook, or their stories, which would be counterproductive to your own healing and theirs. If this sounds familiar based on what you are dealing with right now, flip back to chapters 2 and 3 and consider some of the opportunities referenced there, like single-day volunteer events, answering the phone, or working at a fundraising event. Once you have stopped feeling that every day holds more bad news, you might be ready to work more deeply with others who need your help.

As someone who wears the dual hat of both survivor and volunteer, you will be in a unique position. You will be seen as a leader rather than as part of the client group, but you may still have residual sensitivities of your own. The key to being an effective survivor-volunteer is not confusing sympathy and empathy. In a *sympathetic* reaction, you acknowledge the trauma of others and provide comfort. In an *empathetic* reaction, however, you might have trouble separating your own experience from what the person in front of you is currently going through. Many general descriptions of the distinction between sympathy and empathy conclude that with empathy, you have experienced the same feeling yourself, while with sympathy you have not. But as a survivor-volunteer, you certainly have experienced many of the same feelings. To experience true empathy and "walk in the other person's shoes" might be risky, since you *have* already walked in their shoes and are trying to heal from the experience. Experts in resilience and its impact on healing agree that the real difference between sympathy and empathy lies in whether you can listen to someone else's trauma without taking on their feelings as though they were your own. If you are going to volunteer directly with people who have similar experiences to yours, practice your sympathetic reactions as a way to keep yourself emotionally safe. Ease into the volunteering role and allow yourself time to develop the ability to separate what others are experiencing from your emotions about your own experiences.

Sympathy and empathy are also related to compassion. Compassion is the drive to take that sympathy and empathy and turn them into action on someone else's behalf. You're already interested in doing that, or you wouldn't be reading this book! Trauma survivors have a natural compassion for other people because of their past experiences. We just have to be extra careful not to take on others' suffering as we compassionately reach out to help.

While emotional expressiveness and feeling comfortable with your emotions can be a reflection of how much time has passed and whether you're ready to emotionally engage with others, there are personality types who will never be interested in talking about their emotions, no matter how much time has passed. It's fine to never be interested in the more emotionally expressive types of volunteering. It doesn't necessarily mean you haven't healed; it just means you need to choose carefully which volunteer path will be right for you and the people you want to help.

If you are someone who prefers to *do* something rather than talk about something, you might be the perfect person to consider being a patron or a donor to the cause you care about. Becoming a patron or donor can be a deeply rewarding way to participate. In giving financial support to a cause you care about, you are providing the resources and programs that will help others join you on the path to healing. Donors to nonprofit organizations fund programs that provide face-to-face support and scientific research, and even grant money to people who can't pay their bills during their own crisis.

If you were helped by a specific nonprofit organization during your traumatic experience, you may already know of a group that could use your donation. You might even know exactly which programs helped you the most and how you would like your donation to be used. Even if you were not connected to a specific nonprofit during your experience, there are great resources to help link you up with an organization with goals you can get behind. Your mental health professional or support group might have recommendations, and there are also great lists available online, containing information about various nonprofits and the work they do.

Becoming a donor is a giving-back activity that doesn't require you to be fully finished with the healing trajectory. Nor do you need to be wealthy! According to the "How America Gives" report from the *Chronicle of Philanthropy*, families with the lowest wages give a higher percentage of their income as donations to charity than middle-class or wealthy families.[4] A great way to start getting involved in the nonprofit of your choice is to make a small but meaningful donation, and then over time build a stronger and stronger relationship with the organization. Maybe you make a donation and volunteer at an event in your first year. In the year following, perhaps you increase your donation and find more intensive ways to volunteer. No amount is too small for you to make a difference in the life of someone who is waiting for help to start healing. No matter how you deal with your emotions, there's someone out there who's a perfect match for the help you can give.

Dan is a perfect example of someone who struggled to find the right emotional outlet for his healing. Dan and his wife Mariella felt their world crumble when, thirty weeks into their first pregnancy, they received the news that their baby wasn't going to be able to survive after being born. The child they had waited so long for had a fatal genetic abnormality, and the diagnosis was crushing. Dan and Mariella had a few weeks to process the terrible news and to come to grips with the fact that the baby they could still feel kicking inside her wasn't going to be able to survive outside the womb. During those two weeks, Dan and Mariella did their best to steel themselves for the roller coaster ride of emotions that was to come. They made plans for photographs to be taken in the hospital during the few short hours they expected the baby to live and planned the inevitable funeral service. They gathered the materials to take hand- and footprint castings from their son's tiny body. They spoke to grief counselors about how to cope with the first few weeks. They were as prepared as any couple can be for such a devastating end to a long-awaited dream.

When the baby was delivered at thirty-two weeks gestation, he passed away as expected, but Dan and Mariella had the precious time they needed to capture a few memories.

One of the reasons Dan and his wife confronted the hard work right away is that they knew that couples who go through trauma can sometimes grow apart. Grief has a sneaky way of coming between loved ones, and the grieving process sometimes feels like it's a lone battle. When couples retreat to their separate corners to handle their grief and begin healing, it can be a recipe for marital strife. Dan knew that and wanted to prevent it.

Several months after the loss of their son, Mariella made a donation to the organization that took pictures of their family in the all too brief moments they had in the hospital with their son before he passed away. Mariella and Dan both treasured those pictures, and Mariella wanted to make sure everyone could have such a treasured keepsake. Several months later, the organization invited Mariella to be a volunteer for them. She knew as soon as she went to the training that she was not emotionally prepared to actually be a volunteer photographer; being around other teeny babies who were fighting the same struggle as her late son was too much for her to handle. But she found a great role for herself as the point of first contact for families who were making the same preparations that she and Dan had made. She reached out to them with compassion to set up the photography sessions and followed up afterward when she forwarded their pictures, which had been placed into a lovely album by thoughtful volunteers.

Dan couldn't understand how Mariella could do it. How could she look at pictures of babies every Saturday? Didn't it remind her of their son? Of what they had lost? Mariella thought Dan was just refusing to ever be happy again and refusing to open his heart up to others who were suffering. The two were at an impasse—until one day when Dan found himself in the garage, trying to figure out what to do with the pieces of an old toy box they had purchased for their son. It was too painful for Dan to look at. He wanted to destroy it. As he ran his hands over the soft cedar, a thought occurred to him. He took apart the wooden sides and started to scale them down. He put the hinges back on the top, and gently opened the lid. Dan carried the new, smaller box back into the house and started to fill it with some of the few mementos he had from his son: the hospital blanket, hospital bracelet, a tiny lock of his hair, the hand- and footprint molds, and the photos that had been taken by volunteers in the hospital.

In that moment, Dan realized that he wasn't supposed to provide face-to-face emotional support for other families who were losing or had lost their babies. He would leave that to Mariella and the others. He was supposed to build beautiful keepsake boxes where families would be able to store the treasures from their baby's lives. He would give them a beautiful box they could be proud of, not a cardboard throwaway. He would give the babies a remembrance they deserved. As he sweated over the first dozen boxes in his garage the following weekend, Dan knew he was doing what was right for him. He had finally made sense of how giving back had to fit into his life.

For you to be ready to give back to others, like Dan finally was, you have to come through your emotional struggles, find your emotional footing, and then understand how that plays into your plans to give back. If you are always waiting for the sky to fall, like Chicken Little, your emotional journey may still be happening. And if you don't understand how you deal with your own emotions, you are less likely to help anyone else deal with theirs. It's okay if, like Dan, you don't want to verbally express your emotions all the time, either as part of your own healing journey or as part of giving back to others.

As you travel along the healing trajectory, your emotions will be running high. Now is the perfect time to truly understand how your emotions have played into your journey so that you can harness them for your own benefit and the benefit of others who need you.

Chapter 6

DISCOVERING YOUR VISION FOR HELPING

You've made it to the last section! The question you'll explore in this chapter is the most personal of all the questions, and the most open-ended. The earlier questions were designed to help you better understand how various forces—like the time you've spent healing, your personality preferences, and your style of emotional expression—can play a role in your decision to give back to others. These factors are an important part of figuring out what type of philanthropy experience will be the most comfortable and most meaningful for you. As you come to the end of the healing trajectory, however, one of the last questions you need to consider is one of the most critical of all: What do I feel drawn to do as a way of helping others?

Question 8: In what ways do you see yourself making a meaningful difference?

Throughout the book, we've talked about all the different ways a trauma survivor might feel pulled to give back. You may have decided you are passionate about supporting the newly traumatized or supporting those who are making the transition back into the "real world." You may want to personally dig in and be someone's emotional support system, or you may want to stay a little bit more on the sidelines and provide behind-the-scenes support for an organization. You may want to be an advocate, a founder, a mentor, or a donor.

Remember that no matter what role you choose, there isn't a "best" way to use philanthropy to heal. Giving back to others has emotional and psychological benefits no matter how you choose to do it. For that reason, this chapter focuses exclusively on what you feel is going to be the best path for you, based on what the first seven questions have revealed about yourself and your healing.

By answering the questions in the previous chapters, you have examined your own healing process, your strengths as a potential volunteer, and your desires as they relate to giving back to others. Moving forward, you will be able to make informed choices as a survivor-volunteer. Those choices will enhance your own healing experience, as well as the healing of everyone you help. Before leaping in, carefully consider the questions you have answered in this book so far, and develop a vision for how you want to make a difference in the lives of others. The rest of this chapter is designed to help you make it happen.

Perspective and Expectations

No matter what type of philanthropy you choose, the act of giving back to others will give you the perspective you need to take the final steps on your healing journey. Many of the personal stories of survivorship in this book focus on survivors finding perspective. In the middle of your own crisis, it can be hard to see the needs of others, let alone adapt to accommodate them. As we've explored, when you are deep in the throes of trauma, you're busy taking care of yourself. As you travel further along the healing trajectory, not only are you capable of expending your energy on other people, but you also have a lot to gain by doing so. Working with someone who is just starting on his or her own path to healing will help you realize how far you have come. You will be able to move from a viewpoint where you can only see your own suffering to observing how many other people are sharing your experience. You will come to realize how many other people need your help, and you will discover the strength within you to help them. People all over the world use helping as a part of their healing strategy every day.

At this stage, it is also important to think about your expectations for philanthropy work. You may not always be rewarded verbally for your efforts. Sometimes, the people you will be working with will be so entrenched in their own trauma that they may not show appreciation for your help, or even recognize the service you provide.

One leader of a nonprofit told me a story about a woman, Lillian, who had survived domestic violence and had to move out of her home, quit her job, and start a new life for herself. Lillian was eager to give back to the organization that had helped her get back on her feet, and she became a first-responder volunteer. She was proud of her new role as the first face a woman or man saw when they chose to physically leave their abusive relationship, and she was with them in their most critical moments. But Lillian had unrealistic expectations of how clients would react to her. When Lillian herself had been in her moment of crisis, she was momentously relieved to be out of danger. She expressed deep gratitude to the volunteer who was there at the door to receive her. Imagine Lillian's surprise when, the first time she was on call to bring a woman in to the shelter, the woman responded to Lillian not with gratitude, but with anger!

The idea that a woman who has just left her home, her belongings, her relationship, and practically her entire life might be angry and lash out isn't that far-fetched. Lillian may even have been told during her volunteer training to expect such a reaction. But Lillian had convinced herself that every incoming client would be as grateful to her as she had been to her own volunteer. She had unrealistic expectations for what her job would entail. If she went into that particular volunteer role to buoy her own feelings of being needed, she may have been sorely let down. You must check in with your expectations for your own volunteer work to make sure you are doing it for yourself and not because of how you expect others to perceive you or respond to you.

It's also best not to go into a volunteer opportunity with expectations on the level of work you'll be given. It may take time to work your way up to doing the kind of volunteer work you feel will be the most meaningful. Many organizations request that volunteers—even those who have survived the trauma the organization addresses—learn the ropes by working at a lower level before moving up to some of the more challenging positions.

Remember that some nonprofits have firm requirements about how much time must have passed before a survivor can volunteer. Many hospitals, for instance, require a one- to two-year distance following a traumatic event before a former patient can return as a volunteer. Smaller organizations may have shorter time requirements, or no time requirements at all. We know some of the reasons nonprofits might choose to reserve certain volunteer activities for survivors who have reached the later stages of healing: First of all, survivors who haven't completed the healing process may set back their own healing through inadvertently reliving their own trauma. Volunteers who might work face-to-face with clients in the middle of trauma need to be psychologically solid enough that they don't run the risk of posttraumatic stress when they hear the stories of other people.

Another reason nonprofits might prefer volunteers who are in the later stages of the healing trajectory is that longer-term survivors are less likely to project their own issues and fears onto others. If a survivor is still working through the healing process, that volunteer might have trouble separating his or her own issues from that of the client needing help. A survivor who is in the later stages of the healing trajectory might be less fragile, less judgmental, and have the professional distance required to have tough conversations with clients.

If you don't meet the time requirements for volunteering in the way that you would like, try not to take it personally. Nonprofit organizations created these rules to protect not just their clients but their volunteers as well. The rules have to apply to everyone, and they may not take into account whether you are truly ready earlier than other survivors. Some of the volunteer opportunities can be incredibly intense, and the nonprofits have established the rules not to judge you but to help create a positive experience for everyone. Your preferred volunteer role will be available to you in time.

Your Strategy Is Your Strategy

You may be feeling ready and able to advance your healing by using philanthropy, but perhaps you don't know yet what will be a meaningful service project for you. Don't worry. This is a great time to do research. Ask other survivors from your support groups. Ask friends and family. Ask your support professional. Many communities have foundations or other organizations where several nonprofits are listed, and you can read about your options before you contact any of them. Don't be afraid to try something and have it not feel right—it's common to volunteer for several nonprofits before you feel like you have made a good match.

On the other hand, some survivors may already know exactly how they want to give back to others. They may know of a nonprofit organization that supports their cause and even be very clear about what kinds of activities they are interested in. Maybe their analysis based on the questions posed here aligns exactly with what they've been dreaming of doing. But it's good to be aware that sometimes there can be a mismatch between organization and philanthropist when it comes to doing what you want to do. As we've seen, not all nonprofits work on behalf of a cause in the same way. For example, if juvenile diabetes is the issue you are passionate about, you could choose to volunteer with the Juvenile Diabetes Research Foundation, which raises money for type 1 diabetes research through large-scale events that are held throughout the world. You could also choose to work more directly through a nearby hospital with programs for children being treated for type 1 diabetes. You could choose to start a local support group for parents of children with type 1 diabetes. You could work with a local agriculture nonprofit to create a spin-off program of "healthy, low-sugar cooking" workshops for the recently diagnosed and their families. Just because you may want to tackle a certain issue doesn't mean the path forward is clear; there is a variety of choices in how to go about it. Do your research on all the options within your chosen cause. Just like Lara did in chapter 3, you want to make a good match not just with the cause itself but also with the kind of work you'll be doing and the people with whom you'll be working.

In your search to find the volunteer task that matches you, it can help if you start off by looking at the right kind of organization to begin with. Investigate so you'll understand where the nonprofit organization is in its lifecycle and how that impacts the work being done. In its early stages, a nonprofit needs worker bees to have big ideas, run programs, and create new projects. A brand-new nonprofit is creating itself and needs people who want to do creative work. On the other hand, an older, established nonprofit usually has a ton of staff, and its leaders may balk at a volunteer who approaches them with an idea for launching a new program.

Sometimes individuals align themselves with the largest and most prestigious organization working in a given field—the organization with the big-name draw. But that may not necessarily be the right match for you. Take my area of passion, for example. In the cancer world, you have large, national nonprofits that have been around for decades. A lot of the work they do is global in scope. They may undertake activities like funding research or lobbying for national change. You also have small, community nonprofits that are usually more grassroots. Often, these organizations do work like one-on-one support and providing a hand to hold as a new patient navigates the complicated world of cancer treatment.

Another thing to consider is that different organizations have different priorities. Some organizations lobby governments and institutions for change, others raise money for research, and still others are about psychosocial support. It is important for you, as a survivor, to align yourself with a nonprofit organization that works toward the things you most care about, and then within that non-profit select a volunteer job where you can be passionate about the job you're doing. All too often, survivors get roped into the first volunteer job they are asked to do without realizing that their true passion might be doing something else.

Whether you're high profile or a regular Joe, whether you have plenty of money to share or very little, and whether you have spare time to give or not, you can find a way to give back to others. In many of the examples in the previous chapters, the calling for *what*, exactly, to do seemed obvious. Kate was clear that the rape crisis center was a great place to volunteer before she even called. Michael J. Fox knew that he wanted to fund research to help cure his disease. For other people, the direct connection may not be so clear. In John's case, for example, he didn't necessarily go out looking to help other people. He went to his local veterans center as a client. It was only once he had been helped by them that he realized he could be a helper as well. In Petra Nemcova's case, there were so many ways she could have chosen to positively affect the lives of people who had lived through a natural disaster. She felt most compelled to help the children, however, which is why she focused her foundation on programs that bring stability to children after trauma.

As you prepare to take your first steps into entering the philanthropic world as a trauma survivor, make a smart, conscious decision to do it the right way. You don't need to hide the fact that you yourself are a survivor for fear that others may perceive you as too fragile. Many of the top volunteers at nonprofit organizations have themselves formerly been clients in need.

When a trauma survivor has spent significant time and emotional energy on the healing process, he or she could be ready to make the leap into deeply meaningful service to others. As we discussed in chapter 2, this leap usually doesn't happen until at least six months to two years following the initial event, and it can take longer in many cases. Putting effort into the healing process—like seeking emotional support and being introspective about the traumatic event—can sometimes play a role in helping survivors reach the later stages sooner.

Organizations that are in a position to use former clients as volunteers do so because no one better understands the position of these clients than people who have been there. Volunteers have a chance to connect with people in crisis and serve as a support system.

Get to Know Your Options

How will you decide to leverage your traumatic experience to help others? Consider the following questions:

- If I have made friends within the community of peers who have also faced my trauma, what are those people doing to give back?

- How do I feel about the programs I accessed when I was in the middle of my trauma? Do those programs have needs I can fill?

- Since my trauma, what healing moments have been the most meaningful to me? Do those experiences hold clues to help me find meaningful ways to give back?

Giving "Treasure"

One of the key ways to give back that we talked about in chapter 5 was being a donor. Getting involved by being a donor can be a fantastic tool for anyone at almost any stage of the healing trajectory, and it fills a very great need for the nonprofit organizations. For example, in hospitals, patients often participate in "grateful patient programs," giving gifts of money to support the great work of their medical teams. These gifts not only show gratitude for the hospital but also acknowledge that other people will soon be in a position of need and will be served by the same hospital and doctors. Grateful patient gifts are gifts of thanks, and also gifts that help others who will cross the threshold of that hospital in the future.

If you have been making financial contributions to a nonprofit as you work through the healing trajectory, the later stages can be a meaningful time to make a significant gift. By this time you've probably had a chance to see the organization's programs from the point of view of both a client and a donor, and you may have some strong feelings about a place you would like to make an important donation to that can change the lives of others. Whether you were served by a specific organization or are giving to a cause you discovered after your trauma, your gift as a survivor is especially meaningful. In particular, nonprofits often put special sentimental value on gifts from former clients. Those donations are a reflection that they do their job well from the inside out. By being a survivor who goes on to financially support the institution or the cause that served you, you are changing the future for someone who is following in your footsteps and facing the trauma you have already survived.

Mentorship

Another option for survivors in the later stages of healing is to serve as face-to-face support to people actively in the middle of trauma. You might lead a support group, facilitate a retreat, or be matched one-on-one as a mentor. Volunteer opportunities of this type can be intense, as you will develop a personal relationship with one or several people in the middle of their trauma. The time requirements for this type of volunteering vary based on the nonprofit and the program, but often volunteers need to be available at least once a week. For some one-on-one mentoring relationships, you may find yourself on call at all times in the midst of a client's crisis. Providing face-to-face support of this kind can be incredibly rewarding, because you have the opportunity to watch people start their journey of survival. You will receive real-time feedback from them, and your successes in this type of service won't just be numbers on a page but actual stories of survival from people you have come to know.

When you work as a face-to-face support volunteer, you should expect to receive plenty of support from the nonprofit organization. This type of volunteer is usually highly trained in order to prepare for the intense experience of working with people deeply in the throes of trauma. You should also expect that you might need some support of your own as you do your volunteer work: a shoulder to cry on during a rough day, someone to ask advice of if you are asked a confusing question, or someone to alert if a mentee situation becomes unhealthy or inappropriate. In some nonprofits, this will be the volunteer coordinator; in others it might be the program director. For this type of intense volunteer work, you must make sure to take good care of yourself as well, to continue to be of service to others.

Creating Something New

In many cases, individual survivors go on to found nonprofit organizations or new programs. During their struggle, these people recognized a need that was going unfulfilled. Perhaps the need was for research, perhaps it was for support, or perhaps it was for information. Nationally, nonprofits large and small were founded not just by celebrities but also by regular citizens who faced crises and realized there was something missing. In founding a nonprofit, trauma survivors are crafting from the ground up a solution that they wish they'd had during their struggle. Though it didn't exist for them, the survivor in this position can make sure the solution is there for others who need it. When you start a new nonprofit organization, you are responsible for designing and creating the programs that the nonprofit will deliver. You can construct those programs to meet the needs you identified but didn't have access to when you were the client. Starting a nonprofit can be a fulfilling but challenging way to find meaning after your trauma survivorship. By starting an organization, you are creating an entity that fulfills a need for other people like you and allowing those people to access services they would otherwise be left needing.

One word of caution: In the nonprofit and social sector, there is currently a push for more collaboration and fewer start-ups. The industry has grown by more than 25 percent in the past ten years, according to *The Nonprofit Almanac*.[1] There are about 1.4 million nonprofits already registered with the IRS in the United States,[2] and many nonprofits fail within their first few years. One major focus in the sector right now is the massive duplication of effort that appears to be going on. Potential donors and supporters may resent new start-ups that seem similar to existing organizations. Before considering the need for a new organization, do your homework. Find out if there are any organizations working in that space, doing anything that could be considered similar.

If you start a new nonprofit, one way you can be more relevant and attract more support is by being clearly differentiated from the rest of the market. To achieve this, you must do your research! Know every single one of the nonprofits in your community that work in the subject area. Know what they provide, how many people they service, and how successful they are at it. If you build programs that are like already-established programs, your nonprofit will likely have trouble thriving. Because it is increasingly hard for nonprofit organizations to attract and keep donors, I often suggest that would-be nonprofit entrepreneurs try a slightly different, but still creative, tack. If there is an organization that does similar things but lacks a particular program that you think is a missed opportunity, start a conversation with them about hiring you to develop that program within their existing organization. You'll get a guaranteed paycheck (which you likely wouldn't get if you started a nonprofit from scratch), you'll have some operational stability, and you won't be competing with that organization for donors. In return, they'll get an innovative program and you, a knowledgeable survivor, to run it. You'll still have to do your homework to make sure your program is well researched and viable. By doing so, you will avoid donor fatigue, avoid contributing to an overrun of new nonprofits, and save yourself the costs of starting up a new nonprofit where a similar nonprofit already exists.

If you do decide that starting a new nonprofit organization is necessary to the problem you want to solve, educate yourself on your mission and your clients. The true problems for the majority of clients going through this particular type of trauma may be slightly different from what you experienced. Remember that you are founding this organization to help *them*—presumably you have already gone through your own healing process before tackling the nonprofit start-up venture. Create focus groups of individuals experiencing the crisis, find out what is most important to them, and clearly identify the problems you think your new organization can solve. Though founding an organization will help you, the founder, heal, your mission will always be to reach out to those people who aren't yet as far along on the healing journey.

———

Your entire healing process is unique and personal to you, and never more so than when considering this last question of what, truly, is meaningful for you as a way to give back. When you consider the question of how you will go about making a difference in the world, you are taking all of your experiences up until this point with you. You bring to the table all of your emotions and all of the encouraging words from friends, family, and mentors. You have in your toolkit the ability to leverage your story, if you so choose. You have a unique perspective as a survivor that many other people might need to rely on.

You may find yourself in high demand because you have come

through the fire and emerged a survivor. You could be asked to do many different things for many different organizations that want you to give back to their people in need. The key is for you to discover exactly how you want to do it. If you do it your way, whatever that way is, you will reap the biggest reward—healing yourself and others.

Conclusion

HEALING AND HELPING

By acting as a philanthropist after a trauma, you can strengthen your bonds with the community, make meaning of your own crisis, take action against the very crisis that shook your emotional core, and ultimately rediscover your personal power. Becoming a philanthropist after going through personal trauma is a statement that you refuse to spend your time as a "victim." You are stronger than the crisis that rocked your world, and you will blaze a trail so that others who follow you will have an easier time. As a volunteer, you are stepping into a role as a mentor—and even a hero—to the people who need you.

It is important, however, for you to undertake these helping behaviors in the right time and in the right order. I hope that the activities in this book have helped you uncover—for yourself—the appropriate uses of philanthropy as a healing tool. By taking the time to answer these questions honestly, you have helped to ensure that you select the correct activities that are tailored to your healing phase, personality, and grieving style.

When I was in seventh grade, I met the strongest fighter I would ever know. A newspaper in Texas, based in a town where I had lived and my grandmother still lived, published a small article about a young girl with cystic fibrosis. Kerry was nearly exactly my age, and she was requesting pen pals to write her letters to relieve the boredom of her long days in the hospital. Because of the severity of Kerry's disease, she wasn't allowed to leave the hospital or have any semblance of a life that a twelve-year-old would consider normal. Kerry and I wrote several letters back and forth. She revealed to me that on many days she didn't even have the strength to go down the hall to the community playroom in the children's hospital. But on the days she didn't, the other, younger children came to her. Kerry loved to read, and despite having to struggle for each breath, she greatly enjoyed reading and telling stories to the smaller children who gathered in her hospital room, competing for space among the equipment.

Kerry said that in those moments, she was always eager to show the other children that illness doesn't mean you can't do the things you love, which for her was reading and storytelling. She had a vivid imagination, picturing life outside the walls of the hospital. She painted pictures for the other children of jungles full of animals, castles full of knights, and a life full of excitement. She transported herself and everyone else beyond the whirr of the machines and the tangle of IV lines.

Kerry didn't even realize it, and I didn't either at the time, but she was giving back to those other children. She had a gift of creativity that fed joy into the other children in the hospital with her. She spread her stories and her beautiful pictures of what life could be, and she gave everyone else happiness and hope. Kerry was my first example of graceful giving under the pressure of crisis. Her lessons have stayed with me for decades, even though Kerry succumbed to her cystic fibrosis a few years after our pen-pal friendship began.

Like Kerry, the strongest of us—those of us who have been through the fire of trauma and made it to the other side—have something valuable to offer the rest of the world.

Your personal challenge has given you the potential to contribute great passion and energy to your chosen cause. You have the opportunity to use your voice and your experience as a tool for making change, raising awareness, and reaching others. Your story can actually make the world better for someone else. If you take the time to create a plan for your own philanthropy, as you have done while reading these pages, you will be able to take on the difficult work of inspiring others and lessening pain for people who need your help.

You are ready to take the final step in becoming someone else's hero.

Now, go.

The world needs you.

NOTES

Introduction: Writing Your Own Giving Prescription

1. K. Kaplan, M. Salzer, and E. Brusilovsky, "Community participation as a predictor of recovery-oriented outcomes among emerging and mature adults with mental illness," *Psychiatric Rehabilitation Journal* 35, no. 3 (2012): 219–229; J. Barlow and J. Hainsworth, "Volunteerism among older people with arthritis," *Ageing and Society* 21, no. 2 (2001): 203–217; D. C. Girasek, "Parents of fatally injured children discuss taking part in prevention campaigns: An exploratory study," *Death Studies* 27, no. 10 (2003): 929–937.

Chapter 1: Why Helping Works

1. Stephanie L. Brown, R. Michael Brown, James S. House, and Dylan M. Smith, "Coping with spousal loss: Potential buffering effects of self-reported helping behavior," *Personality and Social Psychology Bulletin* 34, no. 6 (2008): 849–861.

2. Y. Li, "Recovering from spousal bereavement in later life: Does volunteer participation play a role?" *Journal of Gerontology* 62B, no. 4 (2007): 257–266.

3. P. Gutlove and G. Thompson, "Psychosocial healing and post-conflict social reconstruction in the former Yugoslavia," *Medicine, Conflict and Survival* 20, no. 2 (2004): 136.

4. C. S. Shannon and D. Bourque, "Overlooked and underutilized: The critical role of leisure interventions in facilitating social support throughout breast cancer treatment and recovery," *Social Work in Health Care* 42, no. 1 (2005): 85.

5. Y. Li, "Recovering from spousal bereavement in later life."

6. E. Staub, *The Psychology of Good and Evil: Why Children, Adults and Groups Help and Harm Others* (New York: Cambridge University Press, 2003); M. Stein, "Resilience and young people leaving care," *Child Care in Practice* 14, no. 1 (2008): 35–44.

7. Y. E. Balon, K. L. Then, J. A. Rankin, and T. Fung, "Looking beyond the biophysical realm to optimize health: Results of a survey of psychological well-being in adults with congenital cardiac disease," *Cardiology in the Young* 18, no. 5 (2008): 494–501.

8. Stevan E. Hobfoll, Brian J. Hall, Daphna Canetti-Nisim, Sandro Galea, Robert J. Johnson, and Patrick A. Palmieri, "Refining our understanding of traumatic growth in the face of terrorism: Moving from meaningful cognitions to doing what is meaningful," *Applied Psychology: An International Review* 56, no. 3 (2007): 345–366.

9. J. R. Vollhardt, "Altruism born of suffering and prosocial behavior following adverse life events: A review and conceptualization," *Social Justice Research* 22, no. 1 (2009): 53–97.

10. R. R. Greene, S. Graham, and C. Morano, "Erickson's healthy personality, societal institutions, and Holocaust survivors," *Journal of Human Behavior in the Social Environment* 20, no. 4 (2010): 489–506; E. Staub and J. R. Vollhardt, "Altruism born of suffering: The roots of caring and helping after victimization and other trauma," *American Journal of Orthopsychiatry* 78, no. 3 (2008): 267–280; J. R. Vollhardt and E. Staub, "Inclusive altruism born of suffering: The relationship between adversity and prosocial attitudes and behavior toward disadvantaged outgroups," *American Journal of Orthopsychiatry* 81, no. 3 (2011): 307–315.

Chapter 2: Timing Is Everything

1. Richard G. Tedeschi, Lawrence G. Calhoun, and Arnie Cann, "Evaluating resource gain: Understanding and misunderstanding posttraumatic growth," *Applied Psychology: An International Review* 56, no. 3 (2007): 396–406, doi: 10.1111/j.1464-0597.2007.00299.x.

2. M. L. Macvean, V. M. White, and R. Sanson-Fisher, "One-to-one volunteer support programs for people with cancer: A review of the literature," *Patient Education and Counseling* 70, no. 1 (2008): 10–24.

3. R. G. Tedeschi and L. G. Calhoun, "Posttraumatic growth: Conceptual foundations and empirical evidence," *Psychological Inquiry* 15, no. 1 (2004): 1–18; Kelli N. Triplett, Richard G. Tedeschi, Arnie Cann, Lawrence G. Calhoun, and Charlie L. Reeve, "Posttraumatic growth, meaning in life, and life satisfaction in response to trauma," *Psychological Trauma: Theory, Practice and Policy* 4, no. 4 (2012): 400–410.

4. M. J. Schroevers, V. Kraajj, and N. Garnefski, "Cancer patients' experience of positive and negative changes due to the illness: Relationships with psychological well-being, coping, and goal reengagement," *Psycho-Oncology* 20, no. 2 (2011): 165–172.

5. G. Bonanno, *The Other Side of Sadness: What the New Science of Bereavement Tells Us About Life After Loss* (New York: Basic Books, 2009).

Chapter 3: Turning Support into Strength

1. Russ Alan Prince and Karen Maru File, *The Seven Faces of Philanthropy: A New Approach to Cultivating Major Donors* (San Francisco: Jossey-Bass, 1994).

Chapter 4: Telling Your Story—or Not

1. G. Bonanno, *The Other Side of Sadness: What the New Science of Bereavement Tells Us About Life After Loss* (New York: Basic Books, 2009).

2. Ibid.

Chapter 5: Expressing Your Emotions—or Not

1. Richard G. Tedeschi, Lawrence G. Calhoun, and Arnie Cann, "Evaluating resource gain: Understanding and misunderstanding posttraumatic growth," *Applied Psychology: An International Review* 56, no. 3 (2007): 396–406, doi: 10.1111/j.1464-0597.2007.00299.x.

2. Martin Seligman, *Flourish: A Visionary New Understanding of Happiness and Well-Being* (New York: Free Press, 2011).

3. Victor Yalom, "Kenneth Doka on grief counseling and psychotherapy," Psychotherapy.net (July 2010), retrieved from http://www.psychotherapy.net/interview/grief-counseling-doka#section-intuitive-vs.-instrumental-grieving.

4. "How America Gives," *Chronicle of Philanthropy* [data compiled in 2012], retrieved from http://philanthropy.com/section/How-America-Gives/621/.

Chapter 6: Discovering Your Vision for Helping

1. Katie L. Roeger, Amy S. Blackwood, and Sarah L. Pettijohn, *The Nonprofit Almanac* (Washington, DC: Urban Institute Press, 2012).

2. National Center for Charitable Statistics, "Number of nonprofit organizations in the United States, 1999–2009," retrieved from http://nccsdataweb.urban.org/PubApps/profile1.php?state=US.

ABOUT THE AUTHOR

Courtney Clark is the luckiest unlucky person in the world. At age twenty-six, Courtney beat melanoma. But five years post-cancer, routine follow-up scans detected a malformation of the blood vessels in her brain that was close to causing a hemorrhage. The aneurysm, which had shown no symptoms, could have ruptured at any time. Courtney underwent a series of brain surgeries in 2011 to remove the malformation.

Through her young adulthood, Courtney was drawn to working in the nonprofit world both professionally and as a volunteer. She realized as she grew up that others hadn't shared her experienced giving back, and in 2009 she founded Austin Involved as a way to connect young professionals to meaningful philanthropic opportunities. Courtney continued to run Austin Involved during her brain surgeries. Following her recovery, she merged Austin Involved with Austin's Campaign for Philanthropy: I Live Here, I Give Here.

Courtney recently completed her master's degree in philanthropy from Saint Mary's University of Minnesota, where her graduate research became the basis for *The Giving Prescription*. Courtney's favorite part of being a speaker and author is helping people—whether trauma survivors or not—find their own internal resilience and positivity in the face of challenge.

Courtney has been honored with the Leadership Austin Ascendant Award, as well as her high school's Distinguished Alumnae Award. She has been recognized by *Austin Monthly* magazine as one of "20 in their 30s," by *GivingCity Austin* magazine as one of 2012's "New Philanthropists," and by the Leukemia & Lymphoma Society as a candidate for Woman of the Year in 2013. Courtney serves as the board president for Animal Trustees of Austin and is on the board of the Austin chapter of the National Speakers Association. She is a member of the steering committee for Austin's Cities of Service project, and has served on two councils for the Livestrong Foundation, where she represented the interests of young adults with cancer.

Courtney's experience in the community has also helped her grow her family. Soon after launching Austin Involved, Courtney and her husband, Jamie, were at an Austin Involved volunteer day when they met a young high school student with dreams of college and success as a musician. The young man, Anthony, was grateful for the offer of adult support to take his SATs, fill out his college applications, and navigate the world of college entrance. Today, Courtney and Jamie have welcomed Anthony into their family and love when he comes home from the University of North Texas, where he has a scholarship to study classical guitar and serves as president of the Residence Hall Association. Courtney can often be seen proudly wearing her "UNT Mom" T-shirt around Austin.